BARCODE BOOTY

How I found & sold $2 million of 'junk' on eBay & Amazon

And you can, too, using your phone

By Steve Weber

Published by Stephen W. Weber
Printed in the United States of America
Weber Books   www.WeberBooks.com

Author: Steve Weber
Editor: Julie Bird

ISBN: 978-1-936560-06-6

Also by Steve Weber:

The Home-Based Bookstore: Start Your Own Business Selling Used Books on Amazon, eBay or Your Own Web Site

Sell on Amazon: A Guide to Amazon's Marketplace, Seller Central, and Fulfillment by Amazon Programs

eBay 101: Selling on eBay For Part-time or Full-time Income, Beginner to PowerSeller in 90 Days

www.MyBarcodeBooty.com

Contents

ACKNOWLEDGMENTS

Thank you to all the people who graciously donated their time and expertise to contribute ideas, examples, corrections, clarifications and other improvements to this book:

Bill Knauss, proprietor, Bill's Bookshop, LLC.

Brian Freifelder, proprietor, Fivedollarcd.

Chris Green, CEO, FBAPower.

Paul Hanrahan, online bookseller.

Wayne James, proprietor of A Book in Time.

Sue Johnson, online bookseller.

Craig Jones, online bookseller.

Benoit Maison, director, Vision Smarts.

Melissa Miller, author, MyMochaMoney.com.

Janet Langford, proprietor, GrandmaToAbby Books.

Priscilla Ramsey, personal shopper.

Andrew Rigney, FBA seller.

Jeremy Shick, proprietor, ShickWebDesign, LLC.

Cynthia Stine, FBA seller.

Rob Woodbridge, founder, Untether.tv.

INTRODUCTION

One weekend last February, my wife and I packed a big suitcase, put our two children in the car, and drove up Interstate 95 to visit my mother-in-law near Philadelphia. Saturday morning was bitter cold, but to get some fresh air, I took my 5-year-old son for a drive.

Right down the road, before the car had warmed up, I spotted it—a big TJ Maxx store. I hadn't shopped there for 20 years, but recently I'd heard TJ and similar discounters were becoming gold mines for Internet sellers like me. For 10 years, I'd been an online bookseller, and kept so busy with it I'd never thought about selling anything else. But it never hurts to try something new.

We made a quick U-turn, pulled into the TJ parking lot, and backed our minivan up to the front door. Grabbing a shopping cart, we strolled through the door, right past the purses, beyond the bathrobes, and around the skirts. I craned my neck, squinted through my bifocals, and grinned—almost there.

"Toys!" my boy squealed. Or did I say it first? Anyway, it was true—the back shelves were jam-packed with toys of every kind. Hundreds of them! Dart guns, dolls, train sets, miniature china, soccer balls, board games—all marked way below retail. Was it my imagination, or could I see more variety right here than in a mammoth, big-box toy store?

"Looks like Santa had some leftovers this year," I told my son. "Let's look around."

I didn't know where to begin. On the bottom shelf, partly hidden toward the back, was the biggest, most intriguing box in the store. Inside was a giant, remote-controlled robot.

I'd never seen anything like it, and I wasn't prepared for the price—$30, batteries not included. Gulp. I almost threw it back.

"Let's get it, Daddy!" my son shouted. I glanced around at a few raised eyebrows from the older ladies rummaging through the dress racks.

I felt my ears getting red. I caught my breath. The ladies went back to their shopping, and I pulled the phone from my pocket.

"Who are you calling, Daddy?" my son asked.

"Just checking something," I said. After pointing my phone at the barcode on the robot box, my phone emitted a soft "beep" and then displayed its Amazon price, $280. "Holy cow!" I muttered, "I've made about $250, and we just got here."

I dropped the robot into the cart, with the same satisfaction I might get from hitting a hole-in-one, or pulling a slot-machine arm and hearing the jackpot rain down, red lights flashing. But this was no gamble. Thanks to my phone's free scouting app, I knew my likely profit before risking a dime.

The feeling was familiar, but the surroundings were refreshing. In the past decade as a secondhand bookseller, I'd worn out the knees on five pairs of jeans by scooting around in musty basements and moldy attics hunting for books. Here, in a brightly lit room with the smell of perfume, soft music, and friendly people, it hardly felt like work at all.

Diversification is good. For a decade, I'd made my living selling books, mainly on Amazon. I'd developed a knack for spotting valuable books just by looking at the cover. It wasn't foolproof, but on the average day, I could gather up several boxes of books, paying a dollar or two apiece, then resell them for an average of $8 or $10. Now, with a price-scouting app on my phone, I could improve my book-picking tremendously, and expand into toys while I was at it.

And why stop at toys? Now that Amazon has opened virtually all its categories to us independent sellers, I could sell virtually anything. Instead of waiting until the weekend for yard sales or library fundraisers, I could scout for inventory anytime, practically anywhere—Wal-Mart, the pharmacy, the local warehouse club.

This stuff isn't rocket science. You can do it for fun; you can earn a living at it (I do both). That's what this book is about: cashing in on stuff other people have written off as "junk." That's exactly how I stumbled upon the robot (and most of the books I've sold). The bean counters at a big retail chain—perhaps Target or Toys 'R Us—decided those robots didn't sell fast enough, or they didn't have enough left for a big display. So, to free up cash and shelf space, they dumped the rest at TJ Maxx for pennies on the dollar, making the robot cheap and relatively hard to find. That's where I came in. I made the robot easy to find again, listing it on Amazon.com for $380 (yes, $100 above competing sellers). I sold the robot in 10 days—perhaps not fast enough for Toys 'R Us, but plenty fast for me.

Using my phone's scouting app, I found 11 more money-making toys that day at TJ Maxx—vintage Cabbage Patch dolls, last year's Thomas the Train accessories, special-edition Monopoly games. All were in short supply online, commanding $75 to $120, while gathering dust at the back of TJ's, marked down to $20 or $30.

After an hour of treasure hunting, I left the store with my son, who helped me load the van. He'd forgotten about the robot after finding a football jersey (an Eagles McNabb No. 5) and a giant puzzle (marked down 75 percent). Not including those goodies, I'd spent $130 to get $1,000 worth of inventory.

After dinner that evening, I smiled and told a briefer version of my robot story. Some people are amazed to learn how you can earn money using your phone, without even making a call. "Incredible!"

"Just another day at the office," I said, rolling my toothpick.

Then I turned to my wife and said, "Honey, we need to visit your mom more often!" And that, perhaps, was the biggest surprise of the whole weekend.

Getting started

When I started a decade ago, it was simply as a hobby. Selling used books online was, and still is, a good way to get started with e-commerce. I began by selling my own discarded books and was instantly hooked. I continued searching for more secondhand books, reselling them as fast as I could.

My hobby became an obsession. If I did it all day, every day, I figured I'd earn more money than I could at my "real" job. And I was right! Besides, it was fun.

Selling online was a new way to sell old stuff and earn a living. Web stores such as Amazon.com and eBay were growing like crazy, because for the first time, anyone with a PC and access to the Internet and a Post Office could launch a business with global reach.

I'm still doing it. For 10 years, it's been a treasure hunt every day. I get a rush with every big "find," like the time I bought a library's discarded business directory for $5 and resold it on Amazon for $800. (That's what I call "green"—earning 800 clams by diverting a book from the city dump.)

I'm not on old-school book dealer. I don't know much about first editions, collectors' prints, book club copies, or autographs. Learning all that stuff would take several lifetimes, and I don't have that much time. Or brains. So I've kept busy, finding stuff people want to buy. Connecting an obscure book, or an old toy, with someone who's been looking for it halfway across the country—or around the globe—is rewarding. I wrote an entire book about it called *The Home-based Bookstore*.

Now there's a better way to find all sorts of inventory, not just books. As I mentioned in my robot story, scanning barcodes with a scouting app on your phone eliminates the guesswork, errors, and inefficiencies in reselling. The same technology that enables the checkout clerk at your local grocery to effortlessly scan and price your items—instead of pecking numbers on a keypad—is now available for your pocket. Scouting apps show you the exact profit potential of items you're buying. All you need is a smartphone, like an iPhone, Android, BlackBerry, or a pocket computer. You say you don't have a smartphone yet? Well, this is a great time to get one. Android phones are available as low as $100, plus a pay-as-you-go Internet plan costing about $25 a month. Nowadays you don't need to sign a two-year contract unless someone makes you an offer you can't refuse. These costs are a drop in the bucket for active sellers.

This book is about getting started, and about branching out into new things. It's about being a one-person company—making all the decisions, taking the risks, and keeping the spoils. It can be done. You can build a nice business without the hassle of commuting, meeting a payroll, hiring and firing people, or enduring office politics. Or you can get started part-time, earning a nice second income.

I'm not saying it's easy. Get-rich-quick plans are for chumps. Being a secondhand-book dealer, for example, has been hard, dirty work. Driving to yard sales, library fund-raisers and estate sales, crawling around on my hands and knees, looking under tables, rummaging through stacks of dreck, hauling tons of it home. It's grunt work. It's all about finding stuff to sell that costs a dollar or two, and reselling it for $8 or $10. Yet doing it over and over again never gets boring.

Something new comes along every day. Lately I've been learning things from the newer sellers. I'm branching out into toys, games, and household products. Lots of people are doing it; since I started, 1 million new sellers are competing with me on Amazon alone. Some of the smart ones have shared their ideas in this book.

Meantime, thousands of online sellers have dropped out, and they have a laundry list of gripes:

"Nobody buys books anymore."

"It's too competitive nowadays, you can't earn a living."

"Prices are too low, all the 'amateur' booksellers have driven prices down to pennies."

"Bookselling is all in the past, e-books are making books obsolete."

I'll admit, there's a grain of truth in each complaint. Funny thing, though, I heard these same gripes 10 years ago. "Oh, the gold rush is over," they whined.

It's over? Well then, why am I still here, 10 years later, selling more than ever? I can't help wondering whether all the people who have quit were just too set in their ways. Just like every other creature, online sellers must adapt or die.

In my view, there are two basic types of online sellers: the whiners, and the winners. The whiners aren't very good at it, and they spend lots of time feeling sorry for themselves, and looking for someone else to blame. By contrast, the winners don't have much time for carping and complaining—they're too busy making money.

There's still oxygen for this fire. Online sales have increased every year since 2000, according to the U.S. Department of Commerce, which reports increased participation among small businesses and sole proprietors. Even with the sluggish economy during 2008-2010, e-commerce growth continued its double-digit annual gains, partly due to an overall shift away from brick-and-mortar retailing toward online shopping.

More people are going online to buy more of the stuff they consume. And they're not just buying books and videos online anymore, but virtually every category: electronics, groceries, clothing, shoes, jewelry, office equipment. Online, it's usually easier to find what you want, research products, and shop for deals.

If you ask me, the gold rush is just getting started. And the two biggest factors, things I didn't even see coming two years ago, are here now, available to any entrepreneur willing to take advantage:

- **Real-time pricing intelligence for free.** You can use your cellphone to check prices instantly, seeing the price in local stores and nationwide. Free cellphone barcode scanners (I call them "scouting apps") allow you to effortlessly research prices on virtually any item, locally, nationwide, and online. Today anyone with a modern phone can practice retail arbitrage: profiting from price differences in local and global markets. About four dozen such treasure detectors are available free, and I'll explain which ones work best.

- **Fulfillment services.** Big companies have always had this advantage: computerized fulfillment and customer service, and dirt-cheap warehouse space. Lots of them gladly outsource these tasks to a specialist, so they can focus on growing their business and making money. And now, it's available to anybody through programs like Fulfillment by Amazon. In one swipe, you can cut your labor and storage costs while outsourcing 99 percent of the headaches of selling. Believe me, it works wonders for your business, your blood pressure, and life in general. I'll explain how to get started.

These two things are game-changers for online sellers. They enable you to earn more money, sell more stuff, and accumulate less crap. Profitable trading is still an art, but these tools reduce your risk and reliance on guesswork. That's my kind of business plan: recognizing opportunities, and avoiding hurdles that slow you down. It's the difference between treading water and cruising.

To illustrate: With my online selling, I was always able to enlarge my business by simply acquiring more inventory—more secondhand books. It worked OK, but the more inventory I bought, the more rubbish I got, too. When you buy by the ton, as fast as you can, the more time you eventually spend weeding out the crap. Deadwood, I call it. The bigger my business got, the more time and energy was consumed with culling the junk nobody wanted.

Overall, my profits always paid for the deadwood, many times over. But it's a horrifically time-consuming, back-breaking, and sweaty ordeal to go through your shelves, find stuff you've paid good money for, and get rid of it.

Wouldn't it be great, I thought, if I could avoid buying the junk in the first place, or at least keep it to a minimum? If only there were **a tool for predicting an item's profitability** before you bought it, and the rate at which it's likely to sell? Well, that's exactly what these scouting apps do. And you're not limited to selling secondhand stuff anymore. In fact, the most profitable stuff to sell online nowadays is new, unused merchandise that the big, inefficient chain retailers are casting off. Call it what you will—closeouts, discontinued items, remainders, bargain basement stuff. A lot of it is junk, but a lot of it is worth more money now than when it first went on the market.

Deadwood is only half the problem. When you're small, storage costs are a bear. When I started, I lived in a seventh-floor apartment and had a growing family. My "free" storage space was limited. By my second year in business, I was renting a second apartment, plus three Public Storage garages, just to hold my books and shelving. I didn't have any choice if I wanted to get more inventory and earn more profit. But those storage bills totaled $1,900 a month!

I figured I could triple my profits if I could get less expensive ware-house space. And now I have. I've outsourced my warehousing, shipping, and customer service, just like the big boys. My storage costs have fallen from $1,900 a month to $350 a month. Plus, I don't have to pack 100 orders a day and schlep them all to the Post Office every day. All my shipping and customer service is taken care of.

Meanwhile, I've been learning how to buy new inventory in bulk. I get some of my books and toys by the truckload, so I don't have to hand-pick each item anymore. That has freed up more time for finding profitable inventory. But I'm getting ahead of myself. The bulk-buying advice will be at the end of this book.

Sure, selling is more competitive than ever. But the good news is, there are more tools and opportunities than ever, if you're just willing to learn how to use them. For the first time, you can get into business, and have a wizardly amount of market intelligence at your fingertips, with little up-front cash investment. Scouting apps aren't exactly new. They've been around for several years, and booksellers in particular have been buying special hardware and paying hefty subscription fees to use them. Free scouting apps are the game-changer for most people, and they're practical today for the first time, thanks to more powerful phones with auto-focus cameras, and widespread, fast wireless service.

To compete in e-commerce today, you need a combination of tools in your belt. You need a sixth sense, an eye for a good find, a shrewd sense of value cultivated from experience. Combine that with the new tricks in this book and a willingness to learn, and you're ahead of 95 percent of the competition.

But this sounds too good to be true

As I mentioned on this book's cover, I've sold $2 million worth of "junk" on eBay and Amazon. Now, some clarification:

- Grossing $2 million took me 10 years, and required several gallons of elbow grease. Don't think for a minute that this is a get-rich-quick book. The $2 million figure is a gross number, not my net profit. But I'm working on it.

- Was the stuff I've sold really "junk?" Of course not. My customers are thrilled with the stuff they've bought (though it's hard to please everyone) and I'm proud of how I earn my living. But my bread and butter (and what you'll learn from this book) is indeed selling things that have been written off as "junk" by someone else—as closeout, discontinued, bargain-bin, off-price, and distressed merchandise. I know, it seems like a nutty proposition: The best stuff to sell is what other sellers have given up on, have written off as dead money. Well, keep reading.

Why not sell top-of-the-line, brand-new merchandise, like the latest iPods, bestselling books, and this year's televisions? Because the big fish, the nation's biggest retailers, are the biggest buyers and get the best prices. Nobody can compete with Amazon when they're hawking bestsellers at 40 or 50 percent off retail. In fact, Amazon probably loses money on each bestseller. For them, bestsellers are "loss leaders," a method of attracting new customers, who add another thing or two to their shopping cart. And that's where you and I come in, with that hard-to-find item with a sweeter profit margin.

Yes, the "junk" that the big boys have written off is a great opportunity. Sometimes junk is junk, but there is tons of cream out there for skimming.

Do I really think that you, too, can sell $2 million worth of stuff? The only thing holding you back is you. Give it a shot, and let me know how it goes.

— STEVE WEBER

feedback@WeberBooks.com

PURCHASING:

USE YOUR PHONE AS A TREASURE DETECTOR

When I started selling books online, I had to hand-pick each book, based on a gut reaction refined by experience—was the book likely to be valuable, or not? I realized quickly that profitable secondhand bookselling is counterintuitive. Bestsellers were usually money-losers, while the oddball books you'd think nobody would ever want were cash cows. Authors like Stephen King and J.K. Rowling might be millionaires, but you can't give their books away after they're a year or two old. Yesterday's bestsellers go for pennies. But the price on niche books, such as *Miniature Horses; Their Care, Breeding and Coat Colors* go up year after year.

Nowadays, you don't need to guess at the value of a book, or any other product. You just scan the barcode with your phone and see what others are charging for it. More than four dozen free price-scouting apps are available for iPhone and Android users, instantly reporting an item's retail price and the going price in secondary markets like eBay and Amazon's marketplace of independent sellers.

These scouting apps appeal to two types of users:

- Regular shoppers who want to compare products and prices at different stores.

- Resellers on the lookout for items that can be bought and resold at a profit at sites like eBay and Amazon, or at local outlets.

Strictly speaking, most of the free apps mentioned here are "shopping apps." At least that's what they were designed for—they're made for consumers. But used in reverse, they make awesome tools for finding stuff for reselling. So, you can use them as "scouting apps," too.

If you've never seen these apps in action, watch this short video for Scandit, a popular scouting app:

http://www.iscandit.com/video

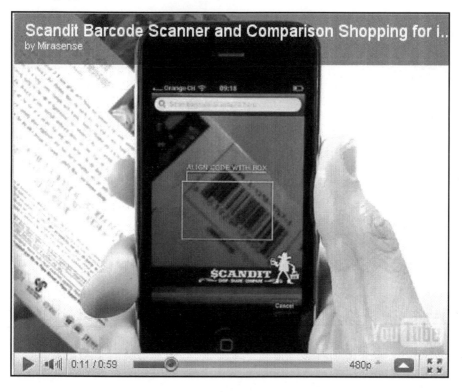

Keep reading for a discussion of which apps are best, and reviews of those designed especially for sellers. The most useful ones provide pricing, the number of competing sellers, and a ranking of how fast the item sells. Developments in this arena are fast and furious, so by the time you've picked up this book, undoubtedly there will be important new things to discover. So, I maintain a website with links to the resources mentioned here, plus new ones as they become available, and a signup form for my free newsletter:

www.MyBarcodeBooty.com.

Chris Green is a power user. He recently walked into a local retail store looking for items to resell on Amazon. Scanning with his phone, he quickly found a couple of new products to resell at nice markups, like this one:

This "Dippin Dots" toy, a frozen-dessert maker, was priced $21.88 in the store, while the lowest price on Amazon was $89.99. Yep, that's a buy. Chris snapped up all he could, 49 of them. Subtracting his Amazon selling fees, he realized a profit of $2,357 on this item. To top it all off, the retail store where Chris bought these toys awards $10 bonus coupons for every $50 spent. So, in addition to his reselling profits, he came home with $210 worth of coupons. His wife had fun with those!

On the same shopping trip, Chris snagged nine radio-controlled toy vehicles for $17.50 each. He quickly resold them on Amazon at $59.95 apiece, netting about $265 on that deal.

Chris might easily have resold his items elsewhere—on eBay, at a flea market, a garage sale, on Craigslist, or a newspaper classified ad. But Amazon is an increasingly attractive, efficient option for third-party sellers of new and used items. A growing army of buyers—100 million U.S. consumers, plus millions more overseas—shop on Amazon because of its vast selection, money-back guarantee, good deals, and convenience. For many shoppers, Amazon's convenience and reliability are even more important than getting a rock-bottom price.

"The convenience of Amazon delivering the product to their door in two days is often worth more than getting the very best price," says Cynthia Stine, a Dallas public-relations executive who sells on Amazon for part-time income. When she's shopping at local stores, Cynthia uses her Android phone to scan for items to resell online. One recent find was a bunch of baby-spoon sets she got for $1.50 apiece at Big Lots, and is reselling on Amazon for $9. Cynthia sends her inventory to Amazon's warehouse, using the Fulfillment by Amazon program. They handle everything from there, and her wares qualify for free-shipping deals.

"People are buying these spoons like crazy, and I'm looking for more because the margins are great," Cynthia says.

Who in their right mind would buy baby spoons on Amazon for $9?

"Probably someone sending a baby-shower gift to someone far away," Cynthia guesses. "Or someone who likes this particular brand, and doesn't want to shop all over the place to find it. Or a man who doesn't know what baby spoons should cost—or maybe it's something else entirely."

A whole lotta scannin' going on

Scouting apps have been around for a while, but they weren't really practical for many people until recently, when phones with fast, auto-focus cameras and fast Internet speed became common. All of a sudden, the apps are hot, partly because retailers have funded their development. Why? Because many regular shoppers who use them buy something directly on their phone, right after they've scanned a product. If retailers like Macy's, Amazon, or Target can get a phone user to use their app, they make more sales.

Meanwhile, more entrepreneurs are using these tools to find deals. ScanLife, which develops scanning services, reported a huge surge in usage during the 2010-2011 holiday season, 16 times the volume of the previous year. According to the company:

- Toys were the most-scanned category, followed by electronics and books.

- Books were the most common item bought by app users who made a purchase on their phone, followed by electronics and housewares.

- The majority of products purchased cost $10 to $30.

UPC Scans: Top Product Categories Scanned & Purchased

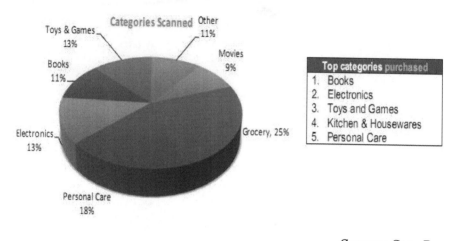

Source: ScanBuy

Scanning has fueled a boom in innovation. Remember Chris Green, the toy reseller? To help find profitable items more efficiently, he developed a specialized app called FBAScout. It displays additional data—not just the online price, but exactly how much inventory competing sellers have, and a sales rank to help predict how fast a certain item sells. Chris sells subscriptions to FBAScout to other sellers, so they can use the extra Amazon sales data, too. It's similar to a tool booksellers have had access to for a few years, but it includes information from virtually every product category, not just books.

"It's the ultimate arbitrage tool," Chris says. "Our users don't just focus on books, we scout for any market opportunity. I've bought things off the shelf at the grocery store and the pharmacy that returned four times their cost within a few days."

I decided to try this myself to see if Chris was making this sound easier than it really is. Sure enough, on my next trip to the grocery store, I picked up the first item I saw on the shelf, a box of Mason jar lids. I scanned, and saw the lids selling on Amazon at twice the price. Impulsively, I bought a dozen boxes. Like I said, don't keep all your eggs in one jar.

Indeed, scanning has gone mainstream overnight. The convergence of four factors—more powerful cellphones, faster wireless speeds, free scouting apps, and the continued growth of online shopping—has created the perfect storm.

At this point, you might be wondering if it's legal to resell products online without any special consent from the manufacturer. Yes, it's perfectly legal, except for a few items restricted by federal or state laws, such as firearms, alcohol, and medical products. For certain categories, such as clothing, you'll need prior permission from Amazon to resell. Otherwise, anyone registered at Amazon who has a U.S. bank account can begin selling just about anything. Just click the yellow "Sell Yours Here" button and follow the instructions. You provide Amazon with your bank account number, and they deposit the proceeds wirelessly. Or you can trade your profits for gift certificates.

Product manufacturers won't necessarily like your online selling, and some of them might even send you a nasty email. (More on this in the "Outlet" chapter in the back of this book.) Otherwise there's not much they can do about it. Items you've purchased at retail are your property; and that's the law: You're free to resell it, give it away, or bury it in your back yard. Certainly, there are exceptions. If you've bought wholesale inventory from a distributor that restricts online sales or advertising, then of course you're bound by that agreement.

Get started scanning. OK, how does this stuff work? Well, scouting apps can recognize a product in two basic ways:

- **Taking a picture.** In this case, you might scan the front cover of a book, a DVD case, a wine label, book, or a poster or artwork. This method works by interpreting the object's shape and written information, which is compared against a list of products.

- **Scanning the barcode.** Similar to the grocery-store checkout aisle, where a small laser records the Universal Product Code found on most products. In some cases, the barcode is an ISBN, or International Standard Book Number barcode, a unique 10- or 13-digit code used to identify books.

Sometimes both of these modes, picture-taking and barcode-scanning, are available in the same application.

Let's take a look at one of several free apps, ShopSavvy, which has 7 million active users and data on 20 million products. You can find it by searching for "ShopSavvy" or "barcode scanner" in your phone's application store.

Launch the app, press the "Scan" button, and align a product bar-code in the viewfinder.

For the best scanning results, follow these steps, which hold true for most free scouting apps:

- Aim straight at the barcode from about 3 inches away.

- Hold the phone steady until the app finds the barcode. If the bars look fuzzy, move the phone a bit closer or farther away to focus.

- For barcodes with two groups of bars, concentrate on the big set of bars on the left. The bars on the right contain only the manufacturer's suggested retail price.

After a successful barcode scan, the app displays the lowest prices for the product, online and at local stores.

Click the "online" tab to see the lowest prices at electronic retailers like Amazon and Half.com, which operate new and used marketplaces. If the online price is higher, you've found a profitable item to resell.

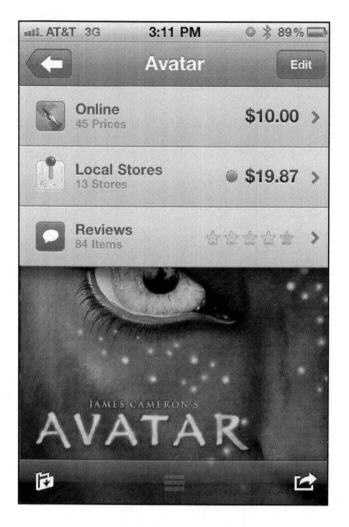

Most people use these apps to find stuff at the lowest price; perhaps they want to see if they can beat their local Best Buy's price by going online. We're using the app in reverse, in a sense—to find cheap stuff locally, which we can resell at higher prices online.

If there are multiple good deals locally, you can get driving directions to the closest stores that stock that item:

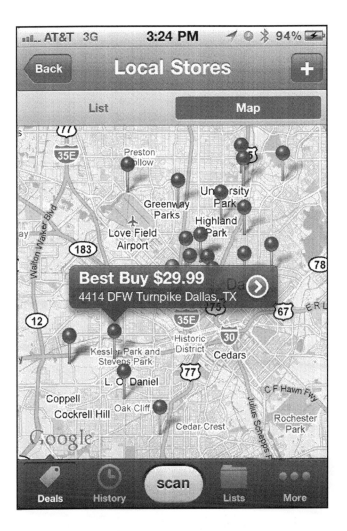

If you purchase the item at a local store, then find a better price elsewhere, you're entitled to a refund at participating retailers.

More features are on the way. ShopSavvy is developing a feature called QuickPay to enable instant purchases of products from within the app. In that sense, ShopSavvy could function as a "virtual wallet" allowing you to pay for purchases at participating online retailers, and even check yourself out at participating local stores.

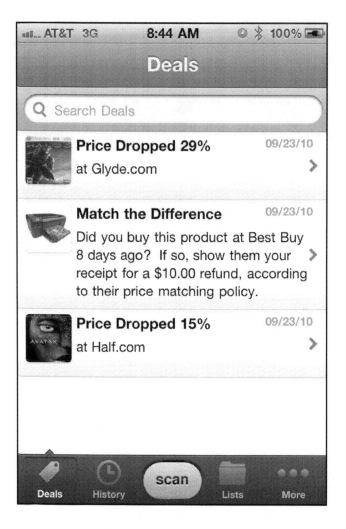

"Our idea is to make it as simple as buying from Amazon—at every retailer," says Alexander Muse, co-founder of ShopSavvy.

Scouting apps are a valuable tool for checking prices and availability on seasonal items. For example, during the holiday season, prices and availability gyrate wildly on merchandise, including toys and other gift items. Some online sellers earn a living by specializing in toys, a fascinating market. Like textbooks, which see huge spikes in demand and prices when new semesters begin, nowadays mass-produced toys are commodities, selling on a real-time exchange that gyrates with the seasons, and with supply and demand.

AT&T	9:50 AM		
‹ Back	**Online**		
All (23)	New (18)	Used (5)	
Amazon Market	Used	$15.00	›
Half.com	Used	$15.74	›
Bookdepository.com		$16.99	›
Amazon Market		$17.75	›
Barnes & Noble		$17.90	›
Amazon		$17.90	›
ecampus.com		$18.48	›
Walmart.com		$18.50	›
Deals	History	scan	Lists	More

For example, during my first year of bookselling, in April I stumbled upon a case of brand-new college nursing textbooks. Scouting apps weren't available back then, and I bought the entire case of 20 books for $10, licking my chops. I figured the books were worth at least $40 apiece, and was calculating my profits in my head on the drive home. When I looked up the textbook on Amazon, I was horrified to see that not only were these textbooks one of the slowest-moving volumes in Amazon's catalog, they were selling for only $5! I couldn't believe my bad luck. But when mid-July rolled around, I got a pleasant surprise. With the fall term just weeks away, those nursing books finally started selling. Each time I sold one, I raised my price by $10. By the time I was halfway through my stock, I was selling three or four a day at $70 apiece, as much as I thought the traffic would bear. Students were happy to pay it, because $70 was still $15 or $20 less than the price they had to pay at college bookstores. Those nursing textbooks taught me a valuable lesson: Have patience when selling seasonal items.

Yes, books and some toys sell briskly all year, while other things sell especially fast—and at much higher prices—during certain times of the year. For example, last summer, I bought 200 copies of a scarce Thomas the Train alphabet-learning toy. It just happened to be available through a book wholesaler I use, and it caught my eye because it was unusually scarce—Amazon had no remaining new inventory, and only a few used ones were listed for sale. I bought all I could at $4 apiece, and offered them for sale on Amazon at $25 each. They sold slowly during the summer, only one or two per month. But by late fall, I was selling several each week. I raised my price to $35, and they sold even faster. It wasn't that popular a toy, but I was the only one selling it because it was discontinued by the manufacturer. Heck, if I'd kept them another year, I might have made twice as much money. But I was willing to take the profit this year, and make all those toy buyers happy. Ho, ho, ho.

That offbeat toy also taught me something about "The Long Tail" of retail, a concept popularized by Chris Anderson of *Wired Magazine*. In a nutshell, it means that niche products, items with little overall demand, can still be quite profitable at Amazon and other big online marketplaces. It's because of the virtually unlimited "shelf space," and the worldwide pool of buyers. Even if consumer demand for something has tailed off sharply—and local brick-and-mortar retailers are unloading the item for pennies on the dollar—you can often resell it for a handsome markup online. It doesn't necessarily matter if there are relatively few remaining buyers for your product; the Internet has efficiently gathered most of them for you.

"Long Tail" products are a profitable niche for online sellers because the big boys can't afford to compete with us. Big stores like Target and Wal-Mart require merchandise that turns over quickly. They carry only the fastest-moving stuff (diapers, T-shirts, Barbie dolls), and move tons of it at tiny profit margins, just a few percentage points. Specialty goods don't work for these behemoths—niche products require just as much warehouse space, but tie up capital far longer. The big stores compete mostly on price, so they must stick with the stuff that moves fast. The rise of Target, Wal-Mart, and Home Depot—and the decline of regional chains, independent hardware stores, and Mom & Pop shops—has only reinforced the trend.

Thirty years ago, at traditional department stores, you could find a little bit of everything. Their motto was "Thick on the best (the most popular products), thin on the rest." By contrast, today's strategy at Wal-Mart and Target is more like, "Thick on the best, the hell with the rest." And the niche products these behemoths ignore are a gigantic opportunity for independent sellers with comparatively low overhead. This leaves the door wide open for smaller operators who deal with niche products that might take weeks or even months to sell, but can be sold at two or three times their acquisition cost.

Yes, markdowns of "the rest" are a gold mine for niche online resellers, and there's more of it every year, says Ellen Ruppel Shell, author of the 2009 business bestseller, *Cheap*.

"Historically, small shopkeepers kept unsold goods on their shelves for months or even years," Shell says. "Today an item that doesn't sell in four or five weeks—or even sooner—may be relegated to the markdown bin."

That's the blessing and the curse for the big boys of modern brick-and-mortar retail. In a walk-in store, it's easy to sell 50 identical jackets at full price, say $90, because the sheer size of the display draws shoppers, Shell says. When only two of those jackets remain, the display is gone. Customers can't find the jackets, and sales stop, unless the price is slashed to $30 (or they're dumped at TJ Maxx). Then, a savvy online reseller can snap up those bargains and sell them online, perhaps for $120 apiece. Online, each jacket has its own display, and the reseller merely waits for one buyer to find each item.

Today's discounting treadmill is common not only in apparel, but furniture, toys, electronics, and books. For example, the brick-and-mortar window for new books nowadays is six to eight weeks. If the book doesn't sell, it's marked down and thrown in the bargain bin. I've sold more than a quarter million books, the vast majority of which I got for 90 percent off retail because they weren't selling fast enough for Barnes & Noble or some other big-box chain.

We'll return to the "Long Tail" again because it's a bedrock principle for online sellers. Another biggie is learning how to sell at higher prices than competitors. Sometimes it requires patience, and sometimes it's all about attention to detail. Remember my story about the toy robot in the introduction to this book? I sold the toy within 10 days, and my price was a full $100 over the sellers competing with me on Amazon. Why would anyone in their right mind buy from me when a competing seller is undercutting me by $100 on the same marketplace? Simple. I have great customer feedback, and it's no accident. I obsess about making every buyer happy—not necessarily because I'm a nice guy, but because I know it's good for business. I've received more than 22,000 customer ratings, and nearly 100 percent of them have given me a five-star rating out of the five possible. Any shopper who glances at my feedback summary knows I'll go out of my way to fix the occasional problem. I also use Fulfillment by Amazon, not only to outsource my fulfillment chores, but to get every possible advantage regarding buyer confidence. The free shipping enabled by FBA, combined with my feedback record, persuades Amazon buyers they'll get the advertised product, with prompt shipping and a no-hassle return policy. That's worth 100 bucks to some people, and a whole lot more to me.

Buy upside-down for profits

Some people use scouting apps both ways—to shop for good deals, and to scout for profit opportunities. For example, Sam McRoberts of Provo, Utah, uses his scouting app to scan books, movies, and video-games—sometimes even commodities such as diapers and baby formula—just to check when the stuff might be cheaper online or across town.

Most often, Sam scans books at shops like the local Barnes & Noble. "I treat physical bookstores as a place to browse for new books to read," he said. "I read a few chapters, and if I like the book, I scan the barcode to see how much it is on Amazon. If the price is low enough, I just order it from Amazon using my phone. If the price difference is small, I might buy it at the local store, so I won't have to wait for shipping."

Other times, Sam uses his phone to scout for inventory at bargain and closeout stores like Big Lots. Here he gets odds and ends for his mom, who resells it on her eBay store, Echix.

A lot of stuff, some of it junky, some precious, is on a perpetual, one-way conveyor belt at these off-price stores. One person's junk is another's treasure, and the way to find the good stuff is scanning. You've probably got a bargain store nearby—Tuesday Morning, Ross Dress for Less, Marshalls, Burlington Coat Factory, TJ Maxx, Big Lots, HomeGoods. More are listed at the end of this book. These places handle what retailers call distressed or expired stock, out-of-season merchandise, "shelf pulls" or salvage. Examples might include last year's clothing styles, or computers or electronics rendered obsolete or unsupported by the manufacturer. These stores handle the items that aren't selling quickly enough to suit the original retailer. That doesn't necessarily mean that people don't want to buy them.

Even the stores known primarily as clothing discounters usually have a constantly refreshed section of bargain-priced books, toys, housewares, appliances, shoes, and other stuff. Even mainstream stores like Target often have a rack or section, sometimes several, devoted to out-of-season or oddball merchandise marked down 50 percent to 90 percent off retail. Sometimes you have to ask where to find it.

Ironically, some of the merchandise brick-and-mortar retailers are desperately trying to unload, at rock-bottom prices, is some of the most profitable stuff you can find if you're reselling it online. Just because the merchandise is discontinued or is a manufacturer's closeout doesn't mean you can't resell it at a nice profit. Sometimes you'll find a special deal simply because the box was dinged. You might be surprised that the most profitable items can be cheesy items like those

"As seen on TV!" gadgets you see advertised on late-night cable TV. Some people will buy anything.

I've found many books to resell by browsing the bargain tables in bookstores, even the ones marked 75 percent off. It's a fun way to spend an afternoon, but it's like finding a needle in a haystack. Most often these books are worthless because the publisher printed way, way too many copies and sales were poor. But once in a while, bookstores throw out the baby with the bathwater. Stores have only so much shelf space, and if the bean-counters at headquarters determine a book isn't selling thousands of copies a year, they usually won't carry it at all. That's one reason it's much easier to find a book on Amazon. So, the right "bargain" book can often be sold online for close to its original retail price, sometimes even more. Remember, though, the law of supply and demand applies, so it pays to scan ahead.

You can find new and used books and many other items for reselling at thrift shops, used bookstores, classified ads, Craigslist, liquidation and bankruptcy sales, yard sales, and estate sales. More on that later. Now, let's shop for more scouting apps:

About three dozen scouting apps are available for the iPhone, and nearly as many for Android phones. The best mainstream consumer apps are profiled in this section, based on my tests in the field with iPhone and Android phones, and input from other users. A separate section in this book is devoted to apps made especially for sellers, most of which are fee-based, and often carry monthly fees, too. For your money, you generally get faster, more extensive data, formatted to enable quick buying decisions. But remember, some of the best things in life are free.

Pic2Shop. One of my favorite free scouting apps is Pic2Shop. Although it's designed primarily for consumers who are comparison shopping, it's well designed and packed with features, which makes it a great utility for sellers scouting for inventory. Pic2Shop:

- Has one of the faster barcode readers among the free apps.

- Recognizes most product barcodes. Many of the free scouting apps work primarily with books, video, and other media, but fail to recognize many other types of products.

- Works on all iPhones and all Android phones, and is available worldwide.

- Displays prices from a wide variety of online marketplaces and local stores.

- Allows you to easily email the scan results. This saves time when you're listing the item for sale online.

Above is the result of a barcode scan using Pic2Shop. Under a small advertisement, you'll see the name of the product and a picture of the item on the left. On the right is a list of online and local retailers who have it in stock, along with their prices. Click on the retailer's name for more information about the product, and prices for the item used. If the item looks like a potential buy, click the "Amazon" link, and scroll to the bottom link, "Amazon.com full site." This will display the regular Amazon product page you typically see on your computer, which contains important data including the sales ranking, product reviews, and competing sellers' listings for new and used copies.

By the way, if you're looking up a book on Pic2Shop, the local-search feature will tell you the closest library where you can borrow a copy.

More than 2 million people downloaded the app in the first year after launch, says Benoit Maison, director of Vision Smarts, the app developer. Most users compare prices while shopping at local stores, perhaps asking for a price match at the checkout counter.

"Also, many people use it to price used items for resale," Benoit told me. "A few people have said they use Pic2Shop to inventory items given to charity. We occasionally hear a funny story, too, like the guy who went around the store where he worked, scanning items, and telling his boss how much he was overcharging!"

For more information:

http://www.pic2shop.com

RedLaser. RedLaser is another free app that shows the price of an item at online and local retailers. Currently it's the best known price-checking app because it was one of the first to be made available free, and it's promoted heavily by eBay, which owns it.

Here's what the app shows after scanning the barcode of a book:

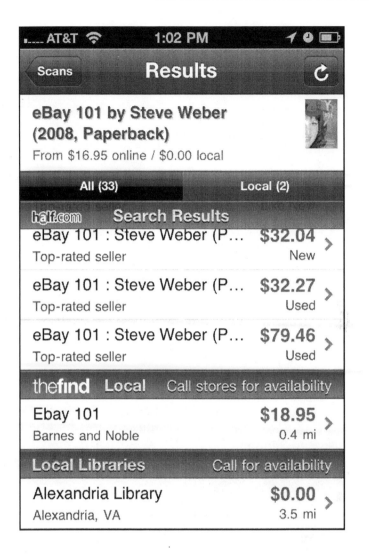

For resellers, RedLaser's best feature is its display of used and new items on eBay and its Half.com division, where independent merchants and individuals can list new and used books, CDs, videos, and games. Half.com is an important source of additional sales for some sellers, but has stagnated in recent years.

You can send your scan results as an email attachment, which can be useful if you have a computerized inventory system. There's automatic search localization for U.S. dollars, euros, and British pound sterling.

RedLaser's major shortcoming is its lack of pricing data from Amazon. The omission is understandable because eBay bought RedLaser in 2010, so the company doesn't want to give any free advertising to its biggest competitor. That's not to say you can't get some use out of RedLaser; it reports prices at 140 brick-and-mortar chains operating 50,000 walk-in stores, which can be a handy reference. The data comes from Milo.com, which also is owned by eBay.

To be fair, Amazon's free scouting app, profiled in the next section, doesn't mention eBay because Amazon doesn't want to generate business for its biggest competitor, either. Fortunately, a growing number of neutral apps, like Pic2Shop, pull pricing data from both marketplaces.

At this point, you might be wondering, "Why does eBay want everyone to know which local stores have the best prices?" Well, for one thing, eBay collects licensing fees from app developers and retailers who use RedLaser's code in their own apps. And, of course, RedLaser generates revenue when it brings shoppers to eBay, too.

eBay expects an ever-increasing amount of its transactions to come from cellphone users, so it's also integrating RedLaser into its other mobile apps including eBay Selling, eBay Marketplace, its Stubhub ticket-reselling site, and Shopping.com.

As mentioned previously, you can find RedLaser (and other apps mentioned here) by searching for the app's name in your phone's application store.

Amazon Price Check. Amazon has its own scouting app, Price Check, which can be useful if you do a lot of buying and selling on Amazon's Marketplace. It's slick and fast, and worth a look.

There are four ways to search using Amazon Price Check:

- **Type It:** Tap this search bar by entering a search term and tapping the Go button at the bottom. This feature is handy if you have, for example, a book with no barcode – just enter some title words and the author name.

- **Scan It:** Tap this button to scan a barcode within the orange indicator arrows. Once the barcode is recognized, the product search is automatic.

- **Snap It:** If you snap a picture of the product, Price Check can usually recognize it by analyzing the image and the writing on the product. It works on books, DVDs, CDs, videogames and even household and grocery items.

- **Say It:** Tap this button to search by spoken words. The app typically usually knows when you're finished speaking, but you can also tap "Done."

The biggest drawback of Amazon Price Check is that it doesn't provide any local pricing at brick-and-mortar retailers. Plus, it keeps pushing you to Amazon's mobile site, which isn't very useful for sellers.

Snaptell. Snaptell is a good utility for scouting for books and other media items for reselling on Amazon. Incidentally, Snaptell was bought by Amazon in 2009, but is still being supported. I believe it's a more useful app than Amazon Price Check because it provides easier access to Amazon's complete catalog details. By contrast, Price Check locks you into using the mobile-phone version of Amazon's site, which omits lots of information useful for sellers.

Another advantage of Snaptell over Amazon Price Check is that Snaptell displays availability and pricing at a few local brick-and-mortar retailers. The biggest drawback: the barcode-scanning is painfully slow.

So it seems that Amazon will continue maintaining both apps, with perhaps Price Check appealing mostly to online shoppers inclined to buy items through Amazon's mobile Web site. By contrast, Snaptell is more suited for resellers because once you've scanned a product with Snaptell, it's easy to navigate to the regular Amazon PC page containing all the marketplace details, including how many sellers are competing to sell, and the Amazon Sales Rank. The sales rank can be a critical factor in your inventory decisions, and is explained in some detail in the next section of this book.

Google Goggles. Remember Sam McRoberts, the gentleman mentioned previously who scans barcodes on stuff that might be good to resell? Well, sometimes he sees something that he thinks might be valuable, but it doesn't have a barcode. That's where Google Goggles comes in. It's a free visual-search app for iPhone and Android that lets you use pictures taken with your mobile phone to search the entire Web for results.

"I'm using Google Goggles to try to identify objects that I think might be valuable, but that aren't easily identifiable," Sam says.

For example, if Sam were at a garage sale, and found a potentially valuable oil painting, Goggles can help him track information about the artist and other works. Sam might not find an appraisal on his phone, but he'd know where to start.

Here's what Goggles spit out after I snapped a picture of my favorite piece of art hanging in my dining room (mine is merely a print, unfortunately):

Goggles also recognized this, one of my vintage vinyl records from the days of disco (yes, I'm old enough to remember, but young enough to keep dancing.)

Like old records, old books tend to be the most valuable, and most don't have barcodes—they didn't appear until the 1970s. But Goggles, like Amazon Price Check, can read the words on an old book's cover, or understand when you speak the title into your phone, no matter what language.

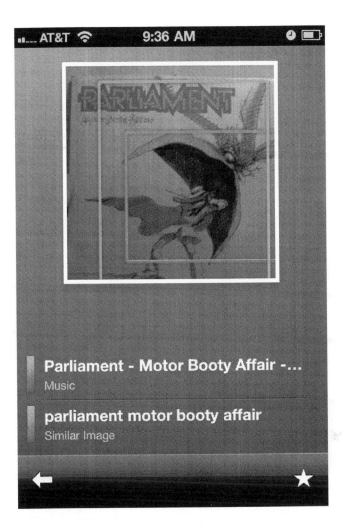

No barcode? No sabe Español? No hay problema.

Some valuable things are hard to put into words. No problem, Goggles has you covered. There's no need to type or speak a query. Just open the app, snap a photo, and read the results.

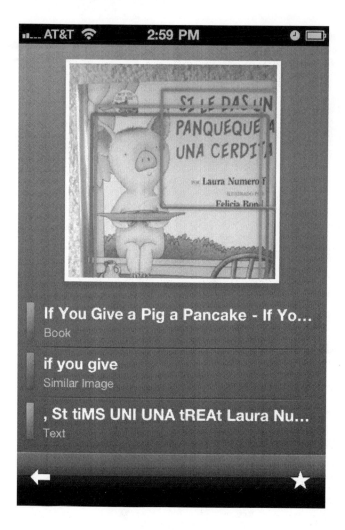

Goggles can even recognize landmarks, such as Wembley Stadium or the Empire State Building. It recognizes most products—it even knew the model number of my six-year-old Yamaha keyboard, just by its shape. But there are limits. Goggles doesn't work very well at recognizing furniture or apparel on sight. Too many variables are in a snapshot of those things.

Google Goggles might not be the most immediately useful app for most sellers, but it bears watching. Anyone involved with the Internet, even tangentially, ignores Google at their great peril.

Getting started with Google Goggles. Goggles is available for iPhone and Android. More information is here:

http://www.google.com/mobile/goggles/

Launch the app, and you'll be guided through a short tutorial. You can start snapping photos or scanning barcodes and check the results.

The search results page will show you Web Results, text matches, similar images, suggested results and offers to translate text.

If you take a picture of someone's business card, you'll get search results for that person, their company's Web address, and often their email and phone number.

Barcode matches send you to a Google Product Search, which lets you compare prices.

You can use Google Goggles to share the photos you've taken through Bluetooth, Facebook, GMail, Android Messaging, or Picasa. From the search results page, just press Menu, then Share Photo.

With Goggles Search History, you can view and manage saved copies of the pictures you take. Your images and the location information of your phone at the time you submitted your image query is saved by Google. You can save up to 1,000 pictures, and if you go over the maximum, the oldest photos in your history will be deleted to make space for new ones. Goggles Search History is unrelated to Google Web History, typically viewed on a desktop computer.

If Search History is disabled, Google doesn't keep any copies of your images.

Currently, Goggles can read English, French, Italian, German, and Spanish. It can translate into those languages, plus Afrikaans, Albanian, Catalan, Danish, Dutch, Finnish, Galician, Icelandic, Irish, Norwegian, Portuguese, and Swedish.

Google Shopper. Google Shopper is an app for iPhone and Android. Essentially it's a stripped-down, easier-to-use version of Google Goggles, designed for comparison shoppers. Like Goggles, Shopper recognizes products by cover art, barcode, voice, and text search. It displays local and online prices, reviews, specifications, videos, and more. You can save items to a "shopping list." You can filter your searches by specific "brands" and "prices."

For resellers, the major draw of Google Shopper is that it automatically recognizes barcodes, and quickly returns product information. Goggles, by contrast, is much slower to use because it requires you to click an icon before it begins processing barcodes—although it provides more searching options.

An annoying tendency of both Google apps is they often steer users toward retailers using Google's online payment system. Those guys and gals at Google are plenty smart, but they still have a lot to learn.

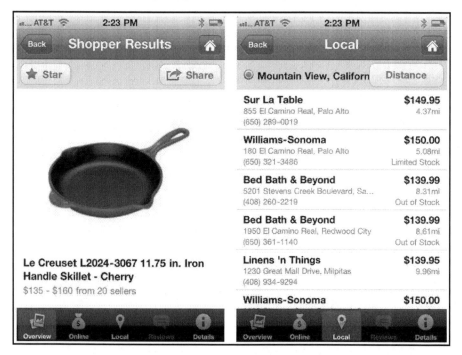

Google shopper is a terrific app for consumers because it collects an enormous volume of product data. But its utility for resellers is compromised because it requires lots of clicking around to find the data resellers want—used prices and sales rankings.

Bakodo. Bakodo is a scouting app that uses the Google Base product search engine, as well as Amazon, eBay, and Best Buy local results. Bakodo's strong points: it scans barcodes very fast, and displays pricing data from many sources. The major disadvantage is that it requires an excessive amount of clicking to navigate among the various data sources. For example, after a Bakodo scan, if you click on "Web results," you'll typically see current pricing on Google Base, eBay, and Shopwiki. You'll see an "Amazon" tab, but no pricing data unless you click on the tab. If you're on a slow connection, and need the Amazon pricing to make a buying decision, this is a major roadblock. Another gripe: this app crashes too often.

A humorous aside: *Bakodo* is the Japanese expression for "comb-over"—a practice of older men who vainly try to mask a balding head. On many such men, the thin, greased strands of tightly combed hair pasted against a light-colored scalp indeed resemble a barcode. Chrome domes of the world, unite!

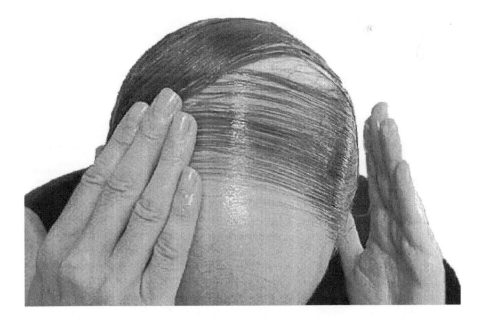

Bakodo is aiming to build a community of users that will suggest new functions for the app, and to rate and review products. The resulting community would allow users to compare reports from friends and other reviewers, enabling better-informed purchases. Users can connect through Facebook to see how their friends have rated the same products. You can post products you scanned directly to your Facebook wall, and even get comments from your friends while you're shopping. These "social" features are fine, but of little use to resellers.

The app links to related ratings from product-research sites Good-Guide, ShopWiki and Stickybits.

Using Bakodo, you can "star" products you want to save for later reference. You can see product detail pages and buy items directly in the application. And you can search for prices in three different currencies—U.S. dollars, euros, or pounds sterling. You can also customize the Amazon store you want to search, directly in Bakodo Scanner (More tab)

Half.com app. Half.com is a trading site featuring an Amazon-like platform where independent merchants sell books, music, and videos at fixed prices, no auctions. Unlike Amazon, Half.com doesn't sell brand-new items itself, although its participating independent merchants can sell new or used books, videos, games, and game systems.

The critical disadvantage of the Half.com app is that it doesn't include any information from the biggest online book marketplace, Amazon.

The Half.com iPhone app includes a barcode scanner for price-checking. Users can also purchase and sell items from Half.com within the app. Scan your item, choose a price, and it appears for sale on Half.com. You can also update the prices on your active listings through the app.

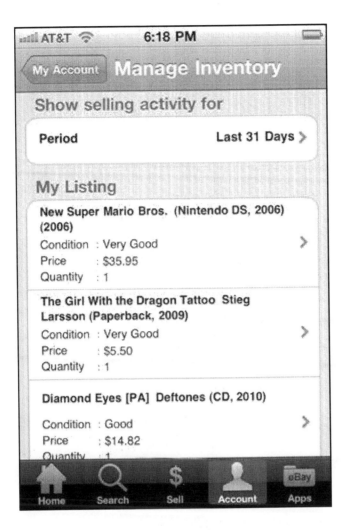

Other features include:

- **Search or browse:** Search or browse for millions of titles in books, textbooks, music, movies, games and game systems.

- **Barcode:** Use the barcode scanner to search for the item you are looking to purchase or sell.

- **Checkout and Payment:** Use your Speedy Checkout setting with Half.com to check out on the go.

- **Manage your active listings:** Edit or delete your current items for sale.

- **Gift Cards and Coupons:** Enter your gift card and coupon codes when checking out to save even more.

Campus Books. Campusbooks.com caters to students looking to buy, rent, or resell textbooks. It can also be used as a free book scouting tool. The free iPhone and Android app works only with book barcodes.

The CampusBooks iPhone app shows online book prices:

AVOID SCOUTING-APP MINEFIELDS

For a variety of reasons, many people who scan don't like to be obvious. One issue is the artificial "shutter" sound that accompanies some applications. The sound mimics the noise emitted by an old-fashioned, motorized film camera snapping a picture. Other apps emit a loud beep when they recognize a barcode, similar to the sound of a supermarket checkout scanner. The sound can be useful for new users who are learning exactly when their application recognizes a barcode. However, the noises can attract unwanted attention in public places like retail stores.

It's understandable that someone in a public place might be annoyed or alarmed if they suspect they're being photographed by a stranger. Indeed, one reason phone makers include artificial camera sound effects is privacy concerns, and the disgusting practice of taking candid, revealing photographs of strangers in public places, which is alarming police and legislators. Congress recently considered the Camera Phone Predator Alert Act, which would mandate shutter sounds to prevent "upskirt" photos, and local jurisdictions are considering such rules. Nationwide, police have been arresting perpetrators using their phones to snap intrusive photos of strangers on escalators, trains, and buses. One arrest occurred in a Wal-Mart.

Scanner and camera sounds can draw the ire of shopkeepers, too. Retailers are nervous when they suspect a competitor is tracking their prices. Years ago, it wasn't unusual for a store manager to ask a shopper to leave if they were observed writing down prices of many items on a pad of paper. That was one way in which cross-town competitors used to keep tabs on competing stores. Of course, with nearly everyone carrying a cellphone these days, store personnel can't realistically ban their use.

So it's a good idea to mute your phone or turn off the sound in your app's settings. If you rely on the sound effects to help you scan faster, try using headphones to prevent the sound from being transmitted through the speakers. If your scouting app uses a flash to aid scanning, you might want to disable that if there's sufficient light.

Even innocent youngsters shopping around with a cellphone barcode app should be careful. Bookseller Paul Hanrahan, who recently loaned his scanner to a granddaughter shopping at a Cleveland library sale, was surprised when the girl encountered hostility from the library personnel. Since then, he has always ensured that the scanner was muted, and now he's shopping for smaller, more inconspicuous equipment.

Library personnel are rightly annoyed by the behavior of some overeager scouts, and their frenetic, boorish behavior has led to outright bans on scanners at some places. Rude scouts, in their zeal to find valuable books, elbow other shoppers out of the way, overturn stacks of books, block aisles, and lay claim to entire rows of books, then dump their rejects on the floor. At two Goodwill outlets in Washington state, customers recently complained to police about a "gang" of booksellers harassing other shoppers, preventing a single book from being touched until the "gang" had scanned it.

So because of the bad apples, some book sale organizers have issued blanket bans on scanners. At some sales, scanners are allowed only on certain days, or during certain hours. Sometimes an extra entry fee is charged to shoppers with scanners. So, check ahead if you plan on traveling to a book sale. And by all means, don't contribute to the bad impression against shoppers scouting apps.

Beware of generic, store brands

One problem with scouting in general is that many in-house store brands, sometimes called "private label" or generic goods, have proprietary barcodes that aren't recognized outside the store's inventory system. In such cases, you might not be able to resell the items online. Most big chain stores have in-house codes solely to enable them to pad their pricing. However, some apps enable users to submit photos, pricing, and details of unrecognized products. So the apps that can generate the most active user bases will improve, and become more valuable for users.

Most apps have weak coverage in two product categories in particular: groceries and clothing. Some small app-makers don't have the resources to display grocery data. Clothing presents even more challenges: Some brands might assign dozens of different barcodes to cover every permutation of a shirt, to cover each possible combination of size, color, and trim. Yet other brands have a single barcode assigned to every variation of a shirt, sweater, or coat.

Barcode reliability is most solid for media items such as books, DVDs, CDs, and videogames. Industry convention demands that a unique code be assigned to every edition or format, like audiobook-, large print, paperback, hardcover, DVD, VHS, hardcover, etc. Also, the barcodes on media items are plainly visible, even when used, because the barcode is printed on the cover or case.

Troubleshooting barcodes and more

The Universal Product Code (UPC) is a barcode symbology widely used in the United States and Canada to track trade items. Each digit is represented by a seven-bit sequence of alternating bars and spaces.

EAN/UPC barcodes were first developed for grocery stores in the 1970s to speed checkouts, reduce errors, and enable computerized inventory control. Their success led to adoption by other product retailers. Manufacturers are identified by the first five numerals scanned in the UPC symbol. The individual product is represented by the next series of numerals. A secret "check code" numeral is added to prevent counterfeit UPC symbols—a method hackers sometimes employ in an effort to get a discount from the product's actual price.

The numerals printed below UPC barcodes function as a backup source for data entry when a machine fails to read the barcode. However, the printed numerals don't include the exact numbers contained in the UPC itself. This is another method to thwart counterfeiters who try to hack the UPC system.

Certain people have been suspicious or fearful of barcodes ever since their widespread introduction a generation ago. Some fringe sects and conspiracy theorists fear barcodes will lead to an oppressive, one-world government; others warn that barcodes have Satanic overtones. In her book *The New Money System 666,* Mary Stewart Relfe claims that barcodes secretly encode the digits 666, the biblical "Number of the Beast" described in the Book of Revelation.

This theory has been adopted by other fringe figures such as the "oracle" Sollog, who refuses to label any of his books with barcodes.

Troubleshooting your app. Unlike the barcode-readers at a supermarket checkout, which use a laser to illuminate the barcode, free barcode apps use the phone's camera and available light (or sometimes a flash). You'll get the best results by avoiding shadows and closing in on the barcode as best as possible. Newer phones, which have auto-focus cameras, work much, much faster.

Like most things, scouting apps aren't foolproof, and occasional glitches are bound to happen. For example, sometimes you might not get any pricing information for a product. Some possible reasons:

1. **Network firewall settings**. The wireless network you are connected to might block your scouting app from accessing the internet. This happens frequently with wifi in office buildings. One way to work around this problem is to switch your phone from wifi to your regular cellphone 3G network.

2. **The product isn't for sale.** If the product is not for sale with participating retailers, then your app might display incomplete results, or no results at all. RedLaser, for example, uses different services to collect price information, including Google and TheFind.com. If those services don't have pricing data, you might not find the product at all.

3. **Your Local Search setting is off.** Sometimes an app won't display local results. Check the app's settings for GPS. If it's set to OFF, switch it to ON.

Seller profile

Janet Langford, GrandmaToAbby Books

Janet is a home-schooling mother, longtime bookseller, blogger, and mentor to several young booksellers.

How and when did you get involved with online selling?

We started out selling on Amazon quite accidentally. I had purchased a few items on Amazon back in the 1990s. I noticed the "Sell Yours Here" button and I was intrigued. What a great idea—after I had read a book, I could "sell it back" to the store I bought it from!

Soon after that, our pet, a sweet Miniature Pinscher, was in an accident and broke her leg in five pieces. The bill from the veterinarian was $1,100. My two young boys donated all their savings, I donated what I could, but we had to raise the rest of the money. That was the birth of our Amazon book business. We paid for the $1,100 bill in a few months, and the rest is history.

A few years later, I read *The Home-based Bookstore* and discovered Amazon Sales Ranks. I invested in three good-quality scanners, and then the three of us became a force to be reckoned with. It moved from being a hobby into a real business.

Now the boys are off at college, and I am paying for their educations by selling on Amazon. My goal is for them to graduate debt-free.

What is your favorite type of product to sell?

It used to be CDs and DVDs because they store so compactly, had great profit potential, shipped quickly via First Class mail, and we could earn extra money on shipping. Since the advent of iTunes, the demand for CDs has weakened. Our favorite product now is textbooks because they sell quickly and are lucrative. I also love books on health, cooking, and Internet commerce.

I like VHS videotapes, also, because they are, by nature, out of print.

How do you decide which items to buy?

It's important to buy low. But don't pass up a valuable book worth $70 to $100 just because you have to pay $25 or more for the book. Sales rank is almost everything. Turning $800 into $3,000 from attending a library sale is better than turning $100 into $400 for the same amount of work.

I use MediaScouter to research prices and ranks.

I would love to triple my investment on every book bought, but will settle for making a $4-5 on any book with a safe rank and a low-enough price.

Are you worried about erosion of sales because of e-books, and diversifying into other types of merchandise?

It is wise to think ahead and diversify, but you shouldn't leave the original model behind. There are still plenty of books out there for those who are willing to work and seek them out.

I still feel that those with a good sales reputation—positive feedback of 98 percent and better—will still be competitive over the long run, no matter how the rest of the book industry goes.

Have you tried the Fulfillment by Amazon program, FBA? Is it viable for your type of business?

Yes, I have tried FBA. After getting through the initial nightmare of listing, labeling, packing and shipping, I was happy with the performance. I do think their software could be much more user-friendly.

FBA puts users ahead of the competition, and using it has changed our buying criteria in a short amount of time.

FIND GOLD AMID CREATIVE DESTRUCTION

Retail is tough, and getting tougher. You might be wondering, "How long can this last? How can regular retailers and product manufacturers possibly survive the cutthroat environment spawned by instant price-checking? Sooner or later, the prices will be cut to the bone, and nearly everyone will be broke, right?

It's not the end of the world. Actually, this stuff is just a new twist on what's been going on forever. Since humans began trading rocks during the Stone Age, commerce has operated on a network of one kind or another. Today, the network is bigger and faster, with lots more moving parts.

Books don't last forever (classics aside) and household products have an even shorter lifetime. Virtually all of them are replaced in a never-ending parade of new refinements, new versions, permutations, and new competitors. More than 500,000 new books are published every year, and the vast majority are money-losers. Nearly 15,000 new grocery items are introduced, and most of them fail, too. Computers and electronics have an ever-shorter product lifecycle. Economists call this the "creative destruction" of capitalism.

Consider the television, for example. A generation ago, there were a few places to buy a set—downtown at a furniture or appliance store. Once you bought one, it wasn't unusual to keep your TV for 20 years—as long as it kept working. Nowadays, you can buy TVs at an electronics store, a grocery store, a big-box discounter, or at any of thousands of online sellers. With new refinements introduced every year—like high definition, three-dimensional displays, Internet access, photo viewing, HD, LED, LCD—some people don't think twice about trading up to a new set every few years. This generates a brisk market for discontinued, refurbished, and used product opportunities, and more profit opportunities for traders.

Retailing will go right on evolving. Inefficient brick-and-mortar operators won't survive. With transparent pricing enabled by scouting apps and other techniques, the built-in advantage of local retailing diminishes. Some retailers are already trying to foil this newer, tougher environment by slapping a custom barcode on products they carry, as a way of thwarting product and pricing comparisons. That might work this year, but not next year.

Scouting apps will keep evolving, too. Online retailers will improve at what they do, or they'll die and make room for somebody else.

"The Internet, and Amazon, moved the individual into the power position when it came to searching and buying discounted products," says Rob Woodbridge, an expert on mobile commerce and founder of the Untether.tv podcast. "But when you stood inside a store, you were ultimately powerless when it came to price-checking. These mobile tools enable the consumer to become more educated about price, feature set, reviews, similar products, and pricing trends. As a result, retailers will have to survive on ever-smaller profit margins, and the value of mid-tier brand names will erode further."

The result: yet more trading opportunities for nimble sellers, and for people who really know their market. "With comparison and discovery engines in the hands of individuals, they can now not only check elsewhere for better prices, they can also see if a cheaper brand with similar features is available," Woodbridge says.

Free scouting apps are surely a revolutionary tool for entrepreneurs and shoppers, and the apps will compete, too, with the better ones getting even better and attracting more users. In the future, more specialized apps will be able to recognize fine collectibles, antiques, artwork, and out-of-print books by the appearance and finish. Developers are hard at work expanding the types of objects that can be recognized. They have some priorities, and must consider basic factors in deciding what type of new objects to support—such as how difficult it is for computers to interpret the object, and the amount of demand for such objects to be recognized.

It's an arms race of sorts, this evolution of trading. Those who can't adapt will die. Entrepreneurs, however, will know this isn't a zero-sum game. They will embrace this new technology just like any other available tool, and create value from it.

Beyond entrepreneurship, there are tons of ways to use price-checking and have fun.

Supercharge your shopping. Let's imagine you're in front of a downtown boutique window, and you see a jacket you'd die to have. But it's Sunday night, and the store is closed. No problem, you snap a picture through the window, and order it online tonight. Retailers using ScanLife allow users to scan barcodes on clothing items and get more details and ordering information. A competing technology from IBM, called Presence, will enable stores to locate registered shoppers the instant they walk into the store, and offer real-time coupons and other special offers.

Purveyors of this new technology promise it will revolutionize retailing. Instead of the frustrating red tape associated with gift cards, wedding registries, and loyalty programs, everything will be right there on the customer's cellphone, personalized for them. This new technology might be an even bigger boon for retailers than it is for consumers.

Find new books. Look up practically any book, and many of the scouting apps will point you to nearest public library with an available copy, using Worldcat, a global card catalog. If you'd rather buy a copy, price-checkers will help you shop from among thousands of online merchants.

You can get reviews of books or other things, like videogames and machines. RedLaser, for example, consolidates reviews from alaTest, which ranks customer approval of games and appliances on a scale of 1 to 100. Some of the apps include Amazon customer reviews, which can be an important factor in your buying decision. For example, one reason that a product might be on clearance is that it has a major design flaw—and Amazon customer reviews will alert you to this.

Sidestep food allergies. Imagine you're allergic to peanuts, and you want to avoid them in that protein bar you've just picked up at the grocery store. Instead of getting out your magnifying glass to read the 500-word list of ingredients, just scan the barcode with RedLaser.

Click "Allergen Info" and the application tells you if there's any pea-nuts—or 11 other typical allergens including gluten, lactose, or soy. You can also get a full rundown of the calories, sodium, and fat con-tent. Nutrition information comes from DailyBurn and FoodEssentials, which cover most name-brand packaged U.S. foods.

Bargain down prices. Let's say you're looking at a bread ma-chine in a department store, and you want it now, but you're unsure if it's worth the price tag of $129. Thanks to your iPhone's built-in GPS location function, you discover that the same machine is on sale for $75 at a store a mile away. Thanks to integration with TheFind.com, you get the bread machine today, and you know you got the best deal.

Let's say you're at Best Buy and you pick up two DVD movies priced at $29.99 apiece. But that's a little steep, because RedLaser tells you the price over at Wal-Mart is $19.99 apiece. Don't feel like driving to Wal-Mart, though? Show the better price to the manager at Best Buy and ask them to match it. A reporter for Money Magazine did just that, and it worked.

Juice your grocery shopping. OK, it's Friday afternoon, you've got a date tonight, and your bottle of mouthwash is empty. Scan its barcode, and it's added to your shopping list on RedLaser.

You can also find special deals, even while you're still shopping. A free iPhone and Android app from the grocery chain Winn-Dixie al-lows you to view the weekly circular and daily sales for that specific store, and create and manage shopping lists that both sync with com-puters and can be shared with other users. More stores are rushing to add these features.

Seller profile: Andrew Rigney:

How did you get started in online selling?

I started selling online back in 1997. My father owned a local marketing business. When my father passed away, I took over his spot, and took the business online. We started out developing custom bean-bag bears in China, and that morphed into selling toys on eBay. This was when eBay was still in its infancy, and not clogged with sellers, as it is now. This was the time when you could actually make money on eBay, and we did!

We sold a lot of different toys, but primarily focused on the Furby, an electronic robotic toy creature. As crazes like the Furby died down, our business fell off and we dissolved the company. A couple of years later, I started a new business making custom bobble-head dolls from China. But I also stayed involved with online buying and selling. I get such a rush finding something in a store that can be resold for a huge margin online. So, while running the bobble-head business, I also continued to scout and resell, and switched from eBay to Amazon.

What is your favorite type of product to sell?

I love toys. In my opinion, they are some of the easiest things to sell. There will always be a built-in demand, because there will always be kids who want them, and parents who are willing to spend money to make their children happy.

Also, I'm starting to branch out into other product areas, like DVDs and books. Also, being involved in Internet marketing, I've become proficient in Search Engine Optimization, and I've developed a number of blogs that refer shoppers back to Amazon, where I can earn an Associates commission.

How do you decide what inventory to buy?

I strongly believe that if you're going to make money on the Internet for the long term, you need to have your fingers in a couple of different pies because one of your revenue streams could dry up at any given moment.

For sourcing inventory, I have a couple of different methods. First and foremost is retail stores. There are so many items on retail shelves that can make you money online. Not only toys, but other areas as well. I travel a lot, so it's easy for me to scout a number of different stores in different areas of the country at any given time. In just the past week, I was able to find three items that I paid a total of $140 for, then sold them on Amazon for $350.

My secondary source of inventory is thrift shops. While it's hard to find new items there, they are a great place to find books, DVD and VHS items. Even if these items are used, they usually have a barcode printed directly on them, so you can scan and research the value.

Why did you leave eBay and start selling on Amazon?

I was one of the first big sellers on eBay, but when it got very popular and flooded with sellers, the profit margins went away, and this gave eBay a "discount" image. I see Amazon's clientele as more sophisticated and willing to pay a higher price, partly because they understand that Amazon backs the products sold there 100 percent, whether it's a product sold directly by Amazon, or third-party sellers like us.

Take a look at any item on Amazon, then look at the same item on eBay. Usually the prices are higher on Amazon by a wide margin. So my online selling is through Amazon exclusively.

What kind of pricing research do you do in the field?

I had been using Amazon Price Check with my BlackBerry. But recently I discovered ScoutPal, a subscription service which provides a lot more information about the new/used marketplace on Amazon. It became a game-changer for me immediately. Using ScoutPal, I've been able to quickly identify profitable items. The Amazon Sales Rank is a big consideration when you're buying inventory, and ScoutPal displays this on every scan.

I pay $9.95 a month for ScoutPal, and that provides access to an offline database I download to my pocket PC, a Dell Axim X51, and I can access online real-time data, too. I use a Microvision ROV laser scanner with the Dell, which cost me $149.

Have you tried Fulfillment by Amazon?

I am just getting started with FBA so I can outsource the shipping to individual customers. Using ScoutPal has enabled me to double my inventory in a short amount of time, so FBA will come in handy, since I don't have the time to personally ship a large number of orders every day.

I have spoken with many FBA sellers, and they have all had a positive experience with it. One seller told me that when he started with FBA, he sent some items to Amazon's warehouse that he had been trying to sell on Amazon over the previous year without much success. As soon as these items went live with FBA and became eligible for free shipping, they sold within two weeks. Amazon's Super-Saver and Prime free-shipping offers are big advantages for sellers. Many buyers will pay a premium to purchase items listed with the "Fulfilled by Amazon" logo.

I haven't converted all of my inventory to FBA, though. I'm continuing to handle the fulfillment of certain items. Since I buy a lot of my items via retail, I don't want them all to be stuck at the Amazon warehouse if they don't turn over. If they don't sell well enough, I have the option of returning some to the store for credit. However, for media items like books and videos, I send them all to the FBA warehouse.

PROFIT WITH RETAIL ARBITRAGE

There's a simple rule for profitable trading: Buy low, and sell high.

Arbitrage is a fancy word used on Wall Street, but it works on Main Street, too. Practicing arbitrage means taking advantage of the price difference between two or more markets. Barcode scanning allows any alert shopper to identify arbitrage opportunities by capitalizing on the difference between fragmented, inefficient local markets, and the global, efficient online market. When you find a bargain on unusual goods in a local store—a pair of Size 16 double-wide shoes, a video-game cartridge for an obsolete machine, an old book on an obscure topic—the local retailer usually discounts these items because they're hard to sell in a local market. The odds are pretty long that someone will randomly walk into the local Five & Dime this week shopping for a hubcap for a 1976 Plymouth Duster—and if they do, they might drive around for another 20 years and never find one. But if they search online, they can find one in a few minutes. And if you're selling one online, you can charge more—exactly what the traffic will bear.

An aversion to haggling. In other societies, price tags are negotiable—no matter the object, the price tag is only a starting point. Here, things are different. Haggling is frowned upon, with the exception of autos, real estate, and maybe certain luxuries. The old saying, "If you have to ask the price, you can't afford it," is gospel to many. Actually, the guy who said it, J.P. Morgan, was filthy rich, and he was talking about yachts. Or maybe it was a Rolls Royce. The point is, the average working stiff paying $20 for something feels obligated to pay "retail," even when he knows the price is inflated. Negotiation is a fight requiring information, confrontation, and confidence. Remember the auto company Saturn, whose main attraction was its "no-haggle" policy? The bottom line is, most people don't like dickering. Nevertheless, Saturn is out of business.

Plenty of people look down on scanning, too, calling it a high-tech version of ticket scalping—a hoarding, profiteering practice that adds nothing to the economy. That's one way to look at it. Ask any Economics professor, though, and they'll agree that transferring goods from a place of low demand to one of high demand is good for everyone. The result is more transactions, a stronger economy, and more choice for everyone. Everyone is happy because they buy and sell at the price they believe is fair.

How to profit from retail arbitrage

By Melissa Miller

Melissa is an online seller at eBay and Amazon. Get more money-making tips at her blog, www.mymochamoney.com

Arbitrage is the practice of taking advantage of a price differential between two or more markets. It's easy if you know the right places to search for items to purchase, then sell for a reasonable profit.

Slickdeals.net. I like to check out Slickdeals.net and browse their Hot Deals Forum, where details of special offers are posted by a community of like-minded deal-seekers. Readers vote on the deals by giving the topic a thumbs-up or thumbs-down. I like to scan the topics with the most thumbs up, and read them first. However, don't discount the items without any "thumbs" because they are newly posted, or perhaps a niche category.

For example, on SlickDeals I found Tony Hawk helmet cameras, cool little cameras for skateboarders, bike riders, and skiers. They were available for $19.99, while they were selling on Amazon for $60 to $80. I purchased as many as I could, then sold them all on Amazon, earning nearly $3,000 in just two weeks.

Using Google Reader, you can monitor SlickDeals' Hot Deals forum here:

http://feeds.feedburner.com/SlickdealsnetForums-9

Another good place to browse is Amazon's "Deal of the Day." Here you'll find brand-new toys, games, books, electronics, and other goods at great prices.

http://www.amazon.com/gp/goldbox/

You can often resell these Amazon "Deal" items at a nice markup on eBay or Half.com. If you don't sell out there, you can wait for the price to go back up on Amazon. More details are here:

http://www.amazon.com/gp/goldbox/

You can subscribe to email alerts for Amazon's Deal of the Day here:

http://www.amazon.com/gp/gss/detail/512430

DealCatcher. I also subscribe to "Deal Alerts" from DealCatcher.com. Here, you enter keywords of products or stores you're interested in, such as Buy.com, Dell, Old Navy, Target, Apple, Sears, and others. Here is the RSS feed for today's deals:

http://rss.dealcatcher.com/rss.xml

For example, I received a recent DealAlert about a Hammacher Schlemmer digital photo converter available at Buy.com for $50. The gadget retails for $200, and a quick eBay search of completed auctions revealed this was a great find. I bought four, and sold them all at a nice markup. Not only that, but the auctions generated lots of traffic to my other eBay auctions and visitors to my website.

If you're an iPhone user, check out the app "TGI Black Friday," which sends you daily updates of coupons and deals from DealCatcher. It's named after the year's biggest shopping day, but it works all year long, giving you advance notice of coupons that appear later in newspapers. See:

http://itunes.apple.com/us/app/tgi-black-friday/id335329737?mt=8

Buy.com is worth monitoring for bargains, too. You can subscribe to receive today's deals from Buy.com here:

http://www.buy.com/todaysdeals/14982.html

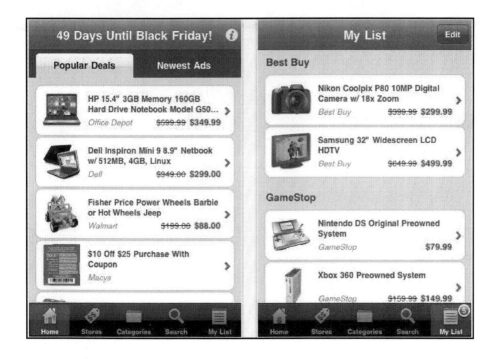

eBay. eBay is a fabulous place to look to find discounted items of virtually any kind, which are often listed by retailers who are clearing inventory. You can purchase these items at a huge percentage off the retail price, then relist them on eBay, Amazon, or any other online marketplace. Many item categories on eBay have a special section for "Wholesale Lots" where you can buy items in quantity and get the biggest discounts.

Craigslist.com. Craigslist.com, the free online classified ads site, is also a great place to look for items that you can resell. Sometimes, the inventory is available free—browse the "free" section under the "For Sale" category. A lot of these items are leftovers from garage sales, or stuff people being cleared out by people who couldn't be bothered to have a garage sale. Using this source, I've found free books, then resold them for good money on Amazon. Other times, I'll buy a box of books listed under the Craigslist "books" category, then resell them individually on Amazon for a nice profit. For the ones that aren't valuable enough to sell individually, I'll group them into categories, such as self-help, health, or business, and auction the lots on eBay.

Local sales and coupons. Local brick-and-mortar stores, especially those offering coupons in the Sunday newspaper, can be a good source of inventory. I've taken many 50 percent-off coupons to my local Michael's craft store, and resold the items on eBay at a markup.

Any retail store advertising a sale, or that has a regular clearance rack, is a potential arbitrage situation waiting for you to take advantage. Even Target stores have permanent clearance shelves, often near the electronics section, near the end of an aisle, facing the wall. Browse these shelves at least once a week.

Take advantage of any coupons, offered online and offline. Often you can combine coupons with a sale price and get fabulous deals. I once found an incredible deal on a Sansa Zune music player at Sears by combining a coupon with the in-store sale price, then resold it on eBay and made a tidy profit. Also, when I've asked, Sears has also matched lower prices offered at online competitors like Costco.com.

Where to sell your items. In addition to Craigslist, eBay, Amazon and Half.com, you can advertise your wares on Facebook or Twitter. You can arrange for payment through PayPal, which is a safer way to handle transactions than dealing with cash.

I have great fun finding things at great prices, and selling them at a profit. There's plenty of room for all of us to do this because the products and places to find them are endless. It's a great way to earn some extra cash from home.

USE ADVANCED SCOUTING APPS & SERVICES

OK, we've seen how free shopping apps can help us find items to resell profitably. Even better tools are available, designed just for sellers, although some of them will cost you. This section examines scouting apps, special hardware, and some subscription services that allow you to work faster and make better buying decisions. These tools can help you build a bigger business, no matter what you're selling.

At the low end, you might simply get an enhanced data service to use with your phone. The next step up would be to connect a high-speed laser scanner to your phone, which is much faster than scanning with your phone's built-in camera. For a top-of-the-line hardware and data service, you might spend more than $1,000 to get a dedicated pocket computer, scanner, and monthly subscription fee.

If you're just getting started, you might be wondering, "Why have the extra overhead of a fee-based scouting service?" Well, look at it this way: If a monthly subscription fee of $10, $20 or $50 enabled you to boost your profits by $2,000 a month, without increasing the amount of time and effort required for your business, would it be worth it? It's a no-brainer, if you ask me.

Some of these souped-up scouting services use special gadgets—instead of using your cellphone's camera to read barcodes, you'll have a faster wireless laser scanner designed just for reading barcodes. But virtually all these services offer a trial period, so you can test them, compare, and judge whether they're worth it. Some services allow you to start with your existing phone, and others will let you rent their hardware on a trial basis. The best services make it very easy for you to try them, because they know you're more likely to subscribe once you see how they'll help your business.

The data services discussed here use catalog, price and customer-demand measurements from Amazon. Not that you need to commit yourself to reselling on Amazon exclusively, or at all. But for wireless scouting, Amazon's constantly updated catalog and pricing data is the best resource for identifying profitable items—and avoiding the unprofitable ones, no matter where you're selling.

Using a dedicated scanner and hardware can be much faster than using free scouting apps like Redlaser. In the time it might take you to check 10 items with a free app, you might check 75 items with Scout-Pal, which is especially tailored for sellers of books, videos, and other media. The volume of stuff you're checking determines how much value you'd get out of these fee-based services. If you're routinely going through stacks of books, videos, CDs and shelves of toys, you'll wonder how you ever lived without one of these specialized services.

It's also possible to pair a wireless Bluetooth scanner with your smartphone, which would boost the speed compared with using the phone's camera to scan the barcodes. One of the smallest Bluetooth scanners available today is the Opticon OPN 2002. It costs about $300 but, as with most high-tech gadgets, prices go down as new models are released. Used models can be had at occasional bargain prices at eBay and Amazon.

Amazon Sales Rank

Before you can appreciate what these advanced scouting apps give you, you've got to understand one egghead principle: Amazon Sales Rank, the touchstone of e-commerce.

I resold used books on Amazon as my full-time occupation for two or three years without ever giving much thought to Amazon Sales Rank. Then, a light bulb went off in my head, and I've never made a buying decision since without carefully considering an item's rank. The Amazon rank allows you to predict how quickly the item is likely to sell on Amazon—and, by proxy, how much demand there is for the item at other online marketplaces and in the economy generally. In other words, an item might be a hot buy if it has a good rank, and a ho-hum buy with a poor rank.

Amazon Sales Ranks are shown in the "Product Details" section of every Web page on the site. To illustrate, there are about 10 million books in Amazon's catalog. The current bestseller has a sales rank of 1, and the slowest seller is ranked 9 million-plus. Many more books have never sold a copy on Amazon, so they don't have a ranking, at least not yet. All sales made through the site, new copies sold by Amazon, as well as used and collectible copies from third-party merchants, figure into the rankings.

You'll find the Amazon Sales Rank for each item about halfway down the item's Web page at Amazon's site. Here's one for a popular book, the rank is displayed on the bottom line:

Product Details

Hardcover: 304 pages

Publisher: Random House (March 1, 2011)

Language: English

ISBN-10: 140006872X

ISBN-13: 978-1400068722

Product Dimensions: 9.1 x 6.3 x 1 inches

Shipping Weight: 1.2 pounds (View shipping rates and policies)

Average Customer Review: ★★★★☆ ☑ (30 customer reviews)

Amazon Bestsellers Rank: #21 in Books

Here you can see the "Amazon Bestsellers Rank of 21. That's a phenomenal rank, only 20 spots back from the No. 1 bestseller. So this copy is selling hundreds or thousands of copies per day, depending on the season. If you list one for resale, priced competitively, it will sell within minutes. At the other end of the scale, one of the slowest-selling books, would have a rank exceeding 9,000,000. It might take five years or more for that one to sell.

I'm mentioning Sales Rank now because it's one of the best features of the fee-based scouting apps described in this section. These subscription-based apps give you effortless access to the rankings. By contrast, the free apps mentioned previously require some clicking around before you see the ranks, which can be an agonizingly slow process.

A side note: Amazon recently began referring to this sales rank system as "Bestseller Rank." But most people still call it "Amazon Sales Rank."

So, the lower the number, the better—the greater the sales volume, and the faster the item turns over. If you list a book for sale with a sales rank of 2,000, for example, you'll likely sell in it within a few hours, because there are perhaps dozens of people buying that book every minute of the day on Amazon.

Sales ranks are dynamic. Amazon recalculates the ranks every hour, depending on the previous hour's sales. So, if a book is mentioned on television, for example, it might zoom up in the rankings for a while.

Amazon ranks are relative, not absolute. The quantity sold isn't publicly disclosed by Amazon, and is subject to seasonal patterns and countless other variables. So, the No. 1-ranked book might sell three times as fast during the Christmas buying season, compared with the dog days of summer, even if it was No. 1 back then, too.

You'll develop your own feel for using the Amazon ranks as you gain experience selling, develop your own philosophy of selling, and specialize in certain areas. For example, if you're a bookseller, you might eagerly acquire a book with a relatively low profit margin, as long as you're confident you'll sell it fast, thanks to the favorable ranking. And you might also be willing to carry a book that sells very infrequently, if you're getting it at a steep discount from the current online price and there are relatively few copies listed for sale.

The rankings involve some guesswork. For example, a rank of 200,000 means that a book sells approximately one or two copies a week, and a ranking of 500,000 might only sell one copy a month—that's my observation. Since Amazon doesn't disclose the sales by title, nobody outside the company knows all the pieces of the puzzle. All we know for sure is, everything else being equal, the bigger the rank number, the slower the sales. And the smaller the number, the faster the sales.

Amazon has different sales rankings for various product categories, too. So, the rankings for home-improvement products , grocery items, games and other categories are separate from the rankings for books, and will affect your buying decision differently. For example, you'd expect a book with a rank of 25,000 to sell fairly quickly—it's relatively close to the top of the 10-million category. But a ranking of 25,000 in Tools is a whole other kettle of fish. For one thing, the catalog is much smaller than 10 million. For another, Amazon's market share in Tools is much smaller. People tend to buy tools at local hardware stores, where they can inspect the item first. Same with jewelry.

Scan your choices. Some of the fee-based scouting services mentioned here aren't wireless at all. Instead, users download catalog and pricing data to a "local" memory card contained in a pocket computer. With this type of system, your price-checking would probably go faster (especially if you have a slow wireless connection), while the data itself might be slightly stale, because it's only updated once a day. The major advantage to local data is that your scouting isn't held hostage if there's no wireless connection, so you can scout for inventory in remote places such as basements and rural areas with spotty wireless coverage. But a local system has disadvantages. The memory cards they use have limited room, so the services can't include every item in the Amazon catalog, meaning you might occasionally miss out on a monster buy if you're using a local system exclusively. And, before you go scouting, you'll have to download a huge file using your desktop computer, which might take 10 minutes or so, even with a broadband connection.

Both types of services have advantages and drawbacks. Some sellers subscribe to both wireless and local services, so they can use either, depending on the situation they encounter while scouting.

Another advantage of the paid apps is that you can configure them the way you like, unlike the free apps, which have few customization options. For example, you might set your paid scouting app to alert you to items you can resell for $20 or more, and ignore items that have an Amazon Sales Rank worse than 400,000. Or you might set the scouting app to beep your earpiece whenever you scan an item worth $50, or anything with fewer than five competing sellers.

All the companies mentioned here that provide specialized scanning equipment and services are small, entrepreneurial outfits. Most of the basic services will work with virtually any phone with a Web browser. They'll work much faster with newer smartphones, and usually even faster with hardware made especially for laser barcode scanning. In most cases, these scouting services were started by people like you and me—innovative, motivated sellers who were looking for a better way to do things. These guys and gals happened to be good with computers and gadgets, and they started selling subscriptions to the tools they originally developed for themselves.

This is not an exhaustive list of service providers. Some, I decided, don't provide a sufficiently broad or up-to-date service. Perhaps there are a few I'm unaware of. A few companies didn't answer my inquiries for this book, so I left them out too. I'm all for the little guy or gal, but I expect them to answer my questions, just like anyone else who expects to get my business or recommendations.

While I'm on my soapbox, this is a good place to mention that I have no personal or financial incentives for including or excluding any particular people, companies, or services here. In other words, I don't, won't, and never have received any fees or commissions from those in this business. I'm not saying it's necessarily wrong to connect a book with affiliate programs, link exchanges, or advertising. I'm just saying, in case you're curious, that I don't.

As mentioned previously, you can view a current list of links to these resources at MyBarcodeBooty.com.

iBookSeller. iBookSeller is a handy, inexpensive scouting app. It costs $2.98 and requires no monthly subscription. After scanning the barcode, it displays Amazon's stock image of the cover, the title, number of new and used offers with lowest prices, and the sales rank—all on one screen, no clicking around required. When I tested this app on my iPhone 4, it functioned as fast as or faster than any barcode-scanning app.

iBookSeller is an incredible value, in my estimation, and a stunning example of how quickly things have evolved in the scouting app arena. Just a few years ago, I was paying $30 a month for a similar data service. Back then, I had to type in the ISBN code manually because affordable, portable scanners simply didn't exist. Yet I was very grateful for that in-the-field pricing knowledge because it enabled me to buy more books at higher prices, with a good idea of their profit potential.

One feature I appreciate with this app is that it automatically illuminates the iPhone's camera flash in low-light situations, ensuring a quick, accurate barcode scan. Currently this app is available only for iPhone, but developer Jeremy Shick told me an Android version is in the works.

Originally iBookSeller got its name because books was the first and most popular category among Amazon third-party sellers. But the app works for any seller—it retrieves the pricing and ranking of other products, too.

For more information:

http://www.shickwebdesign.com/ibookseller.html

Treasure Tester. This Android-only app looks promising, but still has some rough edges. It's a free scouting app, no charge for the basic program or data service.

A nice feature of this app: it notifies you of which items are a "buy" according to the parameters you choose. Unfortunately, Treasure Tester requires the installation of two additional Android apps to enable it to function, an inconvenient and confusing situation. Eventually, I guess this will be fixed with an revised version or better documentation.

Several additional features are being planned for an upgraded, fee-based version of Treasure Tester, which would allow users to see the number of Amazon new and used offers, among other things. An iPhone version is planned, too.

For more information:

http://www.shoplletes.com/products/treasure-tester

ScoutPal. About a decade ago, ScoutPal became one of the first companies selling subscriptions to wireless access to Amazon's catalog, widely known as "Amazon Web Services." It was just about the time that Internet cellphones became popular, eBay was taking off, and Amazon began letting people sell used books on its site. Like most providers, ScoutPal provides both major types of scouting plans: wireless data formatted especially for your phone or pocket computer, and cached information you can download to a hard disk or local memory. Unlike most free apps, which show only limited pricing information, ScoutPal shows lots more data to use in your buying decisions: prices of new, used, and collectible listings, along with the Amazon Sales Rank.

The company offers a numerous options in service levels and hardware. If you wanted to get your feet wet with the cheapest and most basic option, you might opt for "ScoutPal Live," which costs $9.95 a month. iPhone users can access ScoutPal data using their phone's browser, or special configurable versions of the Pic2shop app mentioned previously. For more information:

http://www.scoutpal.com/sp/iphone-redlaser.htm

Android users can use a different app called "Barcode Scanner" as explained here:

http://scoutpal.com/sp/android-barcodescanner.htm

To add more speed, the next step up would be to use a real laser (costing about $400) scanner in conjunction with your phone and ScoutPal:

http://scoutpal.com/db/pdapackage.htm#socket7m

And the next step up would be to use the laser scanner with an HP pocket computer, sold in a package for about $850.

ScoutPal and most other services in this section can be accessed with virtually any cellphone with a Web browser, although if you have an old phone that can't be paired with a scanner, you might have to type in the barcode numbers manually. Current information and details of a free trial are available at Scoutpal.com.

MediaScouter. MediaScouter has been in operation since 2004. It's a local service that places data on your pocket computer or smartphone, so it doesn't require a wireless connection.

Here's an example of a book MediaScouter has flagged as a "buy":

You set MediaScouter with your predetermined scouting criteria, such as price, number of sellers, and Sales Rank. Within a second of your scan, you'll hear a beep if the item is a "buy." This allows you to scan continuously without referring back to the screen. The service is designed primarily for media sellers, who are scanning ISBN and UPC barcodes for books, VHS tapes, DVDs, video and computer games, and music and software.

MediaScouter also has a budget-priced wireless service for Android users called "Pocket Profit," which uses the phone's camera to read ISBN or UPC barcodes and displays the five lowest used and new prices on Amazon, as well as the Amazon Sales Rank.

Like most other fee-based scouting services, there's a free trial available. You can download Pocket Profit and receive 50 free scans to test it. After that, the monthly subscription is $4.99 for unlimited scans. The company also was working on a Windows phone version. For further information, see:

http://m.mediascouter.com/

A laser scanner is also available, pictured below. The Opticon 2002 measures just 1.3 by 2.5 inches, and weighs only one ounce. With a setup like this, you might have the pocket computer in your back pocket, and the wireless scanner on a lanyard dangling from your neck.

FBAScout is a specialized scouting tool designed to appeal especially to sellers using the "Fulfillment by Amazon" program, profiled in the next section. It's available for iPhone and Android.

FBAScout can be used with the barcode scanning apps using the phone's camera, enabling a relatively easy and inexpensive route to getting started. Users can upgrade to a Bluetooth laser scanner as their business grows and they spend more time scouting.

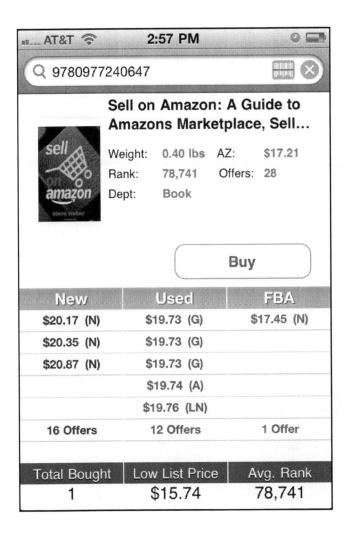

Because it works with virtually any kind of barcode, including tools or grocery items, FBAScout users use it in a variety of ways—for retail arbitrage, book sales, scouting at thrift stores, and closeout merchandise.

FBAScout returns the lowest New, Used and FBA prices for any item on Amazon, not just books and media. It displays the Amazon price, product image, title, weight, category, sales rank, and number of offers. It works with the Scanfob 202 Bluetooth scanner.

The basic service, which allows unlimited scouting, costs $39.95 per month. The company has an add-on service, FBAPower, which can be used to automate the process of listing items for sale through Amazon's FBA program. A repricing service is available, too.

More information is at:

http://fbascout.com.

For more information on the Scanfob Bluetooth scanner, see:

http://www.zerobluetech.com/scanfob-2002-bluetooth-wireless-barcode-scanner/

A last word on scanning. You might be thinking, OK, now I've got all the equipment I need, a scanner, and neatly formatted, current pricing. I'm ready to start printing money!

Not so fast. At some point, you've got to learn the business you're in. No amount of technology is going to help you maximize your business if you haven't nailed down the fundamentals. By that, I mean you've got to pay attention to what you're buying, what's selling, and learn from your mistakes and successes.

Believe it or not, there are lots of people out there with $1,000 scanners who don't know what they're doing. They'll go to a book sale, scan hundreds or thousands of books, but still leave most of the money on the table. If you know books, you can follow behind one of these clowns, and make more than they do, simply picking up their rejects. "Most people don't really know how to read their scanner or what it's telling them," says Craig Jones, an online bookseller. "I've been to book sales with tens of thousands of books, and people with scanners are racing through the stacks at lightning speed, listening to the beeps in their earpiece telling them to buy this book, or not buy that book. I can follow behind these people and find two to five times the inventory they've collected because I understand what I'm seeing on my screen."

To give one example, Craig was at a book sale where he spotted an odd volume that had already been passed over by at least five scanner drones. He snatched it, recognizing its value on sight, and resold it for $1,400.

Yes, it's common sense, but it's also a point that's impossible to overemphasize: Know your business. And, for that matter, don't assume that because a pile already has been cherry-picked that nothing of value remains. Even sellers who know what they're doing have different business models and different criteria. Some flatly rule out books worth less than $5, $10, or even $20. Some pass up books if they have an Amazon Sales Rank worse than 100,000. Books heavier than a few pounds are often shunned. And some sellers totally ignore audiobooks, videos, and music.

Taking your business beyond time and space limits

By Chris Green, FBAScout

Chris Green, a seller on eBay and Amazon for more than a decade, helped develop FBAScout, a subscription service for Amazon sellers. It's similar to book-scanning services that online book scouts have been using for years, but FBAScout specializes in finding any sort of product for reselling, not just books. For more, see FBAScout.com.

When your friends and family find out that you are making extra money (or full-time money) selling on Amazon, they'll often ask, "What do you sell?" For many sellers, the answer has always been books, and sometimes CDs, DVDs, or other media. Getting started with books is easy. They're easy to find, easy to scan, easy to store, and easy to list for sale. You can start a used book business with little to no experience, and very little capital.

With books, competition is fierce. More people are showing up at book sales with scanners. Sources of inventory are finite. Time and space also limit new booksellers—you can spend only so much time scouting for books (especially if you have a full-time job), and part of your time is spent managing the business: listing, pricing, picking, packing, and shipping. On top of this limitation, you can store only a certain number of books before you were forced to rent storage space, adding to your overhead.

Amazon's FBA fulfillment program is a game changer. Now you can outsource your picking, packing, and shipping for very reasonable rates. You can often net more profit per sale, while doing less work. You have more time to scout for more books. Time and space limitations are gone. With FBA, you have access to virtually unlimited storage space, as well as a shipping center that can fulfill as many orders per day as you can generate. Your business can grow as big as you want, and you can get there as fast as you want, with no employees.

And once you start using FBA, it's easy to sell lots of different products, not just books. The supply of used books is finite. Book sales only happen so often each month, and if you live in a small town, they don't happen very often at all. Thrift stores only get so many new books before their whole shelf is penny-book scraps. With FBAScout, you have pricing data for every category on Amazon, not just books.

When people ask me what I do, I tell them I sell online. When they ask what kind of merchandise I sell, I say, "Profitable items." That's really the only criteria I have anymore. Why discriminate? Just find profitable items, and send them to FBA. The categories I deal with most are Books, Media, Toys, and Home Improvement (power tools) because these are the categories I'm most familiar with. If there were more hours in a day, I could branch out into as many categories as time would allow. I'm also considering Amazon's Grocery & Gourmet Food category.

This is a great change in online selling. Many book sellers are right on the verge of seeing this incredible opportunity, if only they can take off their "book blinders." If you are using a scanner and FBA, then you already have 95 percent of this "machine" in place:

- Find profitable items

- Send to FBA

- Profit

- Repeat

Sellers use our service in many different ways: Retail arbitrage, books sales, thrift stores, closeouts, etc. The possibilities are endless when you have no time or space restrictions with FBA and use FBAScout to have pricing data for every item. I've bought items from the grocery store and the pharmacy that returned four times their cost in just a few days.

DIG UP LONG-TAIL INVENTORY LOCALLY

Keep sniffing around, and you'll discover enough local sources to keep you busy.

Supermarkets and drugstores. Today's typical large grocery store carries 30,000 items from the more than 100,000 competing for shelf space. At least 15,000 new snacks, beverages, frozen entrees and other stuff are introduced each year, and four of five fail. To top it all off, retailing is so competitive now that stores are charging fees simply to grant a bit of shelf space to certain products. All this activity creates enormous arbitrage opportunities.

In the personal-care category, for example, it's not unusual to see a $7 box of disposable heating pads selling for $15 to $25 on Amazon. Why? Such manufacturers usually don't have a program for online selling. Some even frown at online sales, thinking it erodes the cachet of their brand, but neither law nor ethics precludes the resale of most stuff. So the opportunity is there for people who are willing to offer these items for sale.

Off-price retailers. Closeout merchandise, including out-of-season and discontinued goods, offers high profit potential for shrewd buyers. This category includes high-volume dealers who work only with established businesses, as well as walk-in stores serving anyone who walks in the door, such as Big Lots, Tuesday Morning, Ross, Marshalls, Burlington Coat Factory and TJ Maxx. Many of these stores, while known primarily for clothing and shoes, also carry an ever-changing assortment of deeply discounted toys and gift items. Just because you see an item marked down in one of these stores doesn't necessarily mean it isn't of value to the right buyer. When you find items still in demand, they can be sold for close to the original retail price, sometimes even at a premium over retail, precisely because the supply is limited. Even cheesy items with the "As seen on TV!" label can garner nice profits.

At these stores, you'll find items such as books, toys, clothing, housewares, appliances and shoes. Sometimes there's a section of items that are deeply discounted to 90 percent off the original retail price.

Wholesale clubs. Includes Costco, B.J.'s Wholesale, and Sam's Club. These no-frills stores have low prices, and make most of their profits from membership fees, which run about $50 annually. These chains, which include local walk-in stores and online buying, can be a particularly good source of toys, tools, and home-improvement merchandise. As mentioned previously, the best source for profitable items will be items marked down for clearance. Deals on clearance merchandise are usually found in the store, not online.

Although these stores call themselves "wholesalers," they're technically retailers because they transact with the public, anyone who buys a membership. However, most of them also offer "business" accounts which can exempt you from paying sales tax, and provide access to advance word of special offers.. To open a business account, be prepared to show your state resale certificate and business license (more on that later).

If you've never researched it, you might be surprised to find how many wholesale clubs are available in your area. Check your local Yellow Pages under "Discount Stores & Clubs" or "Wholesale" to see what's nearby. However, my advice is to ignore the listings for "Dollar" stores, which seldom have items worth reselling.

Library sales. In most areas, library sales are by far the best source of stock for secondhand booksellers. Sales are often conducted monthly, usually on a Saturday, and feature a wide variety of books at very low prices, as well as audiobooks, software, and videos.

Most library sales are organized by a nonprofit Friends of the Library (FOL) group, and most of the inventory being offered has been donated by area residents in very good or like-new condition. Because the library can't absorb most of this material into its collection, the surplus is offered for public sale as a fundraiser. Most books are priced at a dollar or two apiece, and many of them can be sold for $10 or more online. You might also find other media at these sales—audiobooks, videos, and educational materials—at bargain prices.

Sellers who have learned what books to look for can come away from a good-sized library sale with an addition to their inventory worth a few thousand dollars at a cost of $200 or so. And, of course, it always helps to scan the barcode to know the volume's current price and sales ranking.

At bigger sales, the FOL may host a "preview" sale for members only. It's usually well worth the $20 or so in annual dues to get in on the preview sale. Finding one gem will pay for your annual dues, and you'll also have the chance to schmooze with fellow sellers. Get your name on the mailing list of all the FOL groups in your region so you'll know about upcoming sales. The website BookSaleFinder.com also lists upcoming book sales nationwide. If you register at the site, you'll receive periodic emails notifying you of sales in your area.

As mentioned previously some library sales restrict the use of barcode scanners. So it's best to phone ahead, if you're unsure of the policy for the particular sale you're planning to attend.

Many libraries also have a small daily book sale at a shelf or cart near the lobby, and some larger library systems even operate a full-time used bookstore. Sometimes these stores, tucked away in a library basement, are unadvertised gold mines.

In addition to libraries, schools and civic groups organize book sales, and these sales can include some high-quality donated stock. One caveat about book sales in general, however: The biggest and most widely advertised sales aren't necessarily the best places to find good inventory. Sometimes the biggest sales feature a lot of junk left over from the last sale. By contrast, small sales in out-of-the-way locales can be chock-full of great finds but aren't publicized except for a flier on the lobby bulletin board.

Estate sales. Estate sales can be a big source of stock but are more hit-and-miss than library sales. Normally advertised in newspaper ads, these sales liquidate the entire contents of a household and can include large collections of books, videos, music, toys, and collectibles.

If you attend an estate sale, plan on being the first in the door. This can mean standing in line for 45 minutes or more at a well-publicized sale, but getting first crack at the goodies can be worth the wait.

Most estate sales are held on Friday or Saturday mornings. Larger sales may begin on Thursday and continue through Sunday. Remaining items are usually marked down 50 percent on the last day, so a good sale may be worth a second visit. But don't pass up good finds on Friday or Saturday because you think you'll get them cheaper on Sunday. By then, 98 percent of the cream will be skimmed. Get the good stuff while you can.

If there are more estate sales advertised on a given Saturday than you have time to attend, it's worth doing some detective work to determine which sales are likely to have the best items. The newspaper ad should have a contact number for the liquidator running the sale. Phone ahead and ask what types of books are available and how many. Don't rely on the newspaper ad, which might prominently mention "books" among the sale items, when only a dozen cheap paperbacks are available. Likewise, sometimes the ad won't mention books at all, but the estate owner's basement is stacked to the ceiling with collectible volumes. If good books are on sale, try negotiating a volume discount. Instead of $3 per book, for example, ask to pay $25 for 15 books.

If estate sales work well for you, it's worthwhile to cultivate a relationship with the estate liquidators who work the sales in your area. Leave your business card and ask to be notified of all sales involving books. These contacts may also be able to alert you to collections that come up for sale outside the estate liquidation process.

Thrift shops. Thrift shops can be worthwhile for scouting if the store gets new stock often enough. Unfortunately, some charity thrifts like Goodwill stores have begun selling their best donations online. If the stock has been cherry-picked already, it's not going to be worth the time.

Church thrift shops are a potential source of stock too, however. The prices are usually reasonable and the donated items are often of higher quality than those at commercial thrift shops.

Used bookstores. A brick-and-mortar shop can be a profit center for experienced online sellers. Many walk-in stores don't have all their inventory online, and you can find pricing discrepancies. Certain books sell for significantly higher prices online than in a local used bookshop.

Another consideration: items sell for different prices in a brick-and-mortar store compared to online. Arbitrage opportunities abound.

Local retailers. Visit local retailers, speak with the manager, and offer to buy items held in the back room due to slow sales. This can be a valuable source of low-cost inventory when retailers have items they don't want occupying floor space. You can use this same technique at wholesale clubs, thrift shops, and other stores.

Storage unit auctions. Public storage facilities often sell off a variety of belongings after they're abandoned or the owner fails to pay the rent. Usually, the operator allows you to look quickly at the storage unit, then you bid on the entire contents in a public auction. Auctions don't receive much publicity, so it pays to telephone local storage facilities for a schedule. It's pot luck—you can get incredible bargains, and also wind up with a ton of junk using this sourcing method.

Bankruptcy sales and liquidations. Scan your newspaper classifieds for notices of these sales, which can be a valuable source of inventory. Sometimes the smaller, matter-of-fact sales notices are more reliable than splashy, full-page ads, which can be a tip-off that the merchandise is overpriced. For example, in 2009 when the electronics giant Circuit City went belly up and conducted a well-publicized liquidation, an HP printer it had been selling for $150 was priced $270 at the liquidation sale. Meanwhile the same printer was available at a competing retailer for only $135. Yet shoppers stood in line for hours to pay $270 at Circuit City because they were convinced that a liquidation sale must have better prices.

If you're not an expert on an item's price, the only way to be certain is by scanning the barcode and checking competing prices, no matter what the retailer says. For example, a vacuum-cleaner dealer in my town has displayed a going-out-of-business sign on his front window for the past seven years. "Everything Must Go!" the sign screams. The prices are not better than other shops, but the "going-out-of-business" sign must work, because it's still posted, and the store is still open.

MINE BARGAIN INVENTORY ONLINE

No matter how busy your business gets, there's always time to cruise for inventory online. There are lots of websites specializing in "special deals" on everything from Cracker Jacks to hot-air balloon rides. If you don't have closeout stores in your neck of the woods, these deal sites present plenty of reselling opportunities. Here are some of the most popular:

Craigslist.com. This popular website provides free classified ads for local markets. If you poke around here, you'll see lots of people trying to sell their old comic book collections for $50 and up. What you might not have noticed is there's a "free" section in the "For Sale" listings. These folks just have some stuff they want to get rid of. Sometimes they've already put it at the curb, and they're just offering it to anyone who comes by to pick it up. As I'm writing this on a Tuesday morning, my local Craigslist "free" section has 46 fresh offers. People are offering to give away mini-blinds, a dog cage, a humidifier, an upright freezer, a cooler, a 32-inch TV, a 19-inch computer monitor, a collection of Architectural Digest magazines, a waterbed frame, two Mac computers, a laser printer, copy machine, a lawnmower, Monopoly game, stereo headphones, a treadmill, computer desk, an Izod jacket, and other odds and ends. Most of this is stuff you can sell, if you're the one who picks it up, dusts it off, and offers it at a fair price.

If you use Craigslist and you're an iPhone user, check out the CraigsPro app. It has a nice interface for browsing ads and posting to Craigslist. Also, the app lets you run automatic searches of Craigslist for certain items, and sends you the results via "push" notifications, similar to voicemail alerts. You can search multiple cities, view a map browser, search results with photos, and more. For more information, see:

http://itunes.apple.com/us/app/craigspro-craigslist-search/id332324766?mt=8

And there's a free version of the app, which doesn't include push notification and search agents:

http://itunes.apple.com/us/app/craigspro-free-craigslist/id313917737?mt=8#

Two similar offers are available in the Android Market: "Craigslist" and "Craigslist Browser."

Liquidation.com. This online marketplace auctions commercial surplus inventory and government surplus assets. Bulk lots are sold by the truckload, pallet, or small package, and conditions range from new in a box to customer returns and used. Categories include apparel, computers, electronics, housewares, industrial equipment, vehicles, and much more. Warehouses are in Bentonville, Ark., Plainfield, Ind., Fullerton, Calif., Garland, Texas; and Cranbury, N.J.

Salehoo.com. This site lists 8,000 companies offering to "drop-ship" products to fill your orders. You can list the products wherever you want, on Amazon, eBay, or your own website, and the company you sign with fills the order and handles the shipping. It's one of the largest wholesale directories on the Internet and one of the first to offer international wholesale contacts.

Alibaba.com. Founded in 1999 in Hangzhou, China, Alibaba enables buyers and suppliers around the world to do business online through three marketplaces: a global trade platform (www.alibaba.com) for importers and exporters; a Chinese platform (www.1688.com) for domestic trade in China; and, through www.alibaba.co.jp to facilitate trade to and from Japan. In addition, Alibaba.com offers a transaction-based wholesale platform on the global site (www.aliexpress.com) geared for smaller buyers seeking fast shipment of small quantities of goods.

eBay.com. Many sellers earn a living practicing eBay arbitrage. Here's how it works: Inexperienced or careless eBay sellers often auction items and fail to attract bidders because of several typical problems: They haven't taken a competent photograph of the item, or they haven't written a compelling product description. In some cases, auctions fail to attract bidders because they end early in the week or near a holiday, when fewer people shop on eBay. Sometimes an auction is hidden simply because the seller misspelled the name of the product—so savvy resellers regularly search eBay for common misspellings.

Whatever the reason, if an auction doesn't attract enough bidders, the door is wide open for a smart bidder to walk away with a bargain suitable for resale. For example, on a recent Monday at 11 p.m. (when traffic on eBay is relatively light) the unused toy train set pictured below auctioned for $26. Meanwhile, the same item was listed on Amazon at an average price of $97.

You can also "save" your favorite eBay auctions to receive alerts via email whenever certain items are listed.

Yet another way to work eBay into your reselling system is to shop eBay for bargain-priced gift cards. They're often available at a significant discount from the face value. Gift cards from specialty retailers, especially at higher denominations, often have higher discounts. For example, a $432 card from Patagonia, a maker of outdoor clothing, recently sold on eBay for $363, a discount of 16 percent from the card's face value.

Also, eBay has special sections devoted to "wholesale lots" of merchandise in dozens of categories. You can look for deals on everything from a bagful of sunglasses to a truckload of mattresses. Here's how to shop for wholesale lots on eBay:

1. From eBay.com, click "Categories" in the upper left corner.

2. Scan the list of categories. For the ones you're targeting, click the bottom link, "More."

3. When wholesale lots are for sale in your selected category, you'll see a link for "Wholesale Lots." Click through there, and you can sort the list by subcategories, location, and other criteria.

Woot.com. Electronics, kitchen wares, and tons of other stuff. Great discussion boards. Woot sells one item per day until it sells out. A typical example, a factory-refurbished Panasonic camcorder for half the retail price of a new one. Amazon bought the company in 2010 but says it will remain independently operated.

Yugster.com. Similar to Woot but specializes in electronics. A typical example: A "Rock Show Club" toy for $25.

Groupon.com. One deal per day, which are sponsored in local markets. If a predetermined number of users sign up, the deal becomes available. Typical offers are for health, beauty and fitness products and services.

Overstock.com. A wide variety of brand-name merchandise at very low prices and low shipping fees.

SmartBargains.com. Not as extensive a selection as Overstock, but you'll find famous-name products at 30 percent to 65 percent off retail.

JacobsTrading.com. JTC, in business for 40 years, is a direct source for many retailers' and manufacturers' customer returns, overstocks, shelf-pulls, and damaged goods. This company is a true wholesaler, unlike many so-called "wholesalers" who advertise on the Internet, luring beginner entrepreneurs. JTC sells only by the truckload to discount and surplus stores, flea market vendors, auctioneers, and online wholesalers and retailers. Single-category loads consist of "as is" products no longer sold at retail. A load generally consists of one of the following categories: furniture, domestics, tools and hardware, apparel, cookware, electronics, rugs, and appliances. Warehouses are in Appleton, Minn.; East Flat Rock, N.C.; Las Vegas;

Marlin, Texas; Mexia, Texas; Minneapolis; Salamanca, N.Y.; Sneads, Fla., and Taft, Okla.

FatWallet.com. This site aggregates special deals from different Web merchants and presents them in browsable categories.

Milo.com. Milo displays inventory available at local brick-and-mortar retailers. The company's main objective is to allow those traditional stores to compete against online retailers like Amazon, and it pitches itself to retailers as the "Anti-Amazon." The theory is that if shoppers are aware of a decent deal available for immediate pickup in a local store, many shoppers would rather buy the item immediately at the local store, rather than buying online and waiting for the item to be shipped.

Of course, entrepreneurs can also use Milo to scout for bargain inventory. An example might be a local retailer that is closing out a line of merchandise, or having a going-out-of-business sale, or a bankruptcy liquidation. Using this scouting method, it's possible to find inventory to be resold at a profit. eBay bought Milo in 2010 and has integrated its search results into its RedLaser smartphone app.

Google has a competing service called "Blue Dot Specials." When you do a Google product search, blue dots appear beside items available at local stores. Another site, www.thefind.com, performs similar functions.

SCORE WHOLESALE BOOKS, VIDEOS & TOYS

Publisher overstocks and returns from book and toy retailers can be a profitable source of inventory for online sellers.

The book industry is loaded with opportunities for savvy resellers. Each year, about 20,000 books go out of print and about 25 million books go to the bargain bin, becoming what the industry calls "remainders" or "bargain books." When sales begin to slack off for a given title, big bookstore chains return much of their inventory to publishers for credit. Since publishers aren't in the business of selling individual books, they unload the remainders for pennies on the dollar. But just because remaindered books didn't sell fast enough for the chains doesn't mean you can't make money with them. You'll need to research which of the available titles remain reasonably steady sellers and are still worth half their cover price online.

The advantage of adding this type of merchandise as a sidcline is the potential for expanding volume and profits. However, you must research the available titles beforehand to avoid buying titles that are too common online and priced low.

I believe that dealing in closeout, overstock and off-price merchandise in quantity is a good business model, and here's why: Think about the labor involved in finding items to resell. Let's say you're scanning the closeout rack at your favorite inventory source. For each item you find that's suitable for reselling, you've spent travel time, plus more time researching the price and competition. Making a buying decision takes yet more time. Your profit margins might be good, but there is time and labor involved with each item.

Now, suppose that for each buying decision, you can buy multiple pieces of each item. Instead of buying only one copy of a book, or one set of paintbrushes, perhaps you could buy 150. And, what if you could find these items online and have them shipped directly to you, instead of having to travel yourself, and haul the stuff home?

After all, there are only 24 hours in a day. Hunting down sellable items in disparate locations requires time and energy, which are finite resources. If you can develop sources of products in bulk (preferably in a line of merchandise you know well), you can diversify your business, and increase your volume. For example, after I had been selling used books for a couple of years, I branched out into "bargain books" or "remainders," which are available in various quantities from online wholesalers. After some months, this additional type of merchandise became a lucrative sideline to my original used-book business, and eventually the lion's share of my trade. It took me a while to get my footing, and I might never have gotten the hang of it without prior experience selling many thousands of individual books after hand-picking and visually inspecting each one—sometimes called "one off" sales.

So, the potential advantage of buying overstock and closeout items in quantity is that your winning buying decisions can be multiplied. If you find a great item to resell, you can sell it 100 times or more, if you find that many available. But remember, things go wrong when you least expect it. If too many competing sellers buy the same "bargain" as you've found, prices will crater if supply outweighs demand. The downside of buying in bulk is that your mistakes are multiplied, too. Instead of chucking the occasional dud that doesn't sell, you might become saddled with deadwood, and run short of cash.

In his book *What to Sell on eBay and Where to Get It*, author Chris Malta cautions that liquidated products are liquidated for a reason. "No company will ever liquidate a product that has any kind of reasonable resale value to them," he says. If a manufacturer or wholesaler, with all its connections, decided something was a poor seller, that item might be a loser for you, too.

So it's important to understand exactly what you're getting. Pay attention to how such items are described, such as:

- **New.** Mint condition, still in the box, and suitable for retail sale. Although "new," these items might be last year's model, perhaps a few years older, and no longer worth the original retail price.

- **Overstock.** Usually means new merchandise that wasn't sold for some reason. The manufacturer or distributor got stuck with too many, and they want to clear out the floor space.

- **Used.** These items have been returned by stores after the box was opened by a consumer. Often these items are defective or missing a part. For example, a sweater might have a missing button; a toy might have a broken piece.

- **Returns.** Usually means the same thing as "used." The retail packaging has been opened, and the item might be defective.

- **Refurbished.** These items may have been broken by a consumer, returned to the manufacturer, and inspected and repaired. These items might not include the original retail packages, owner manuals, or warranties.

- **Shelf pulls.** These items didn't sell quickly enough at a retail store, and were cleared out to make room for new merchandise. They might have been used as a floor sample, and no longer have the original package.

- **Salvage.** Usually broken or damaged, and only suitable as a source of parts to repair other merchandise.

It's important to understand what you're getting because liquidated merchandise is usually offered "as is" with no warranty, and sales are final. As Chris Malta also points out, there are many online advertisements for "liquidated" or "overstock" merchandise. In many cases, the stuff is of dubious quality—junk that you won't be able to resell. Purveyors of this stuff prey on inexperienced merchants looking to make a fast buck.

So, when you're buying inventory sight unseen from a new source, you should investigate the seller first. To play it safe, limit your trade to established companies with a track record. And remember, transactions can go wrong at well-known, generally reputable companies, too. For example, one of the most famous online brokers of products from China, Alibaba, admitted in 2011 that some of its sales staff helped

2,300 vendors defraud buyers for two years. Although it was a tiny proportion of its transactions, the company has already paid nearly $2 million in claims from the scandal. For the traders who were ripped off, this was a big deal, and some were probably wiped out.

My hunch is that the scammers at Alibaba attracted several inexperienced online sellers who should have known better. According to a report from the company, the scammers purported to be selling current, high-demand consumer electronics at very low prices, with a low minimum-order requirement. The fraudulent transactions averaged about $1,200, and no merchandise was delivered. In other words, the offers were obviously too good to be true, but a constant stream of suckers took the bait each time.

The following outlets usually transact only with businesses, not the public. So be ready to show your state resale certificate exempting your purchases from state sales tax. Minimum orders of $100 to $250 are customary.

Bookazine Overstock LLC

www.bzovoverstock.com

A wide assortment of remainders and "hurts" (new books that have suffered some cosmetic damage) in all categories. New titles are added every day. Order individual titles or skids of assorted titles.

American Book Company

www.americanbookco.com

Remainder and overstock books, including hardcover fiction and nonfiction, children's, cookbooks, coffee-table books, audio, trade formats, and hurt skids. This company has associations with Penguin Putnam, Harper Collins, Abrams, and Brilliance Audio.

Bargain Books Wholesale

www.bargainbookswholesale.com

Remainders, hurts, and closeout books. A variety of categories, with emphasis on children's books, cookbooks, collectibles, crafts, home improvement, inspirational, religion, and transportation.

Book Depot

www.bookdepot.com

Perhaps the widest selection of any remainder distributor, within tens of thousands of titles. Books in all categories, including fiction, nonfiction, children's, audio, and religion. Order through the website or at the warehouse.

Bradley's Book Clearance

www.bradleysbooks.net

A bargain book wholesaler dealing in current hardcovers, paperbacks, and mass-market books. Specializes in African-American, history, mass-market, and New Age. Also carries book-related items such as journals, diaries, bookmarks, book covers and magazines.

Daedalus Books

www.daedalusbooks.com

Remainders in every subject, including the arts, children, history, house and home, nature, and science. Also carries music, specializing in jazz, blues, world, classical, and opera. Wholesale discount requires minimum $200 purchase.

East Tennessee Trade Group

www.rhinosales.com

Specializing in children's, cooking, craft, and home improvement books. Also carries large assortments loaded onto pallets.

Fairmount Books Inc.

www.fairmountbooks.com

Remainders and publishers' overstocks. More than 4,000 titles on all subjects, including children's books, fiction, cooking, gardening, reference, history, and health.

Great Jones Books

www.greatjonesbooks.com

More than 3,000 titles in literature, history, art, architecture, philosophy, social sciences, and more. Now carries a selection of general-interest trade books and children's books. New titles added weekly.

J R Trading Company

www.jrtradingco.com

Remainders, returns, and bargain books. No inventory catalog is published, but the company sends an email and fax inventory list when available.

Marketing Resource

www.mribargains.com

More than 2,500 remainder and overstock titles. Subjects include children's books, gardening, cooking, art, travel, crafts, history, biography, reference and Christian books. Also carries stationery and related closeout items.

Reader's World USA Ltd.

www.readersworldusa.com

Wholesale supplier of books and general merchandise with more than 5,000 remainder titles in stock.

S & L Sales Company Inc.

www.slsales.com

Remainder wholesaler of adult fiction, nonfiction, and children's books. No minimum order.

Tartan Book Sales

www.tartanbooks.com

A division of the Brodart library supply company, Tartan offers recycled library edition hardcovers. Bestsellers and other popular titles are available by the title or in bulk. Shipping for small orders is $2.20 for the first book and 75 cents for each additional book, with special rates for bulk orders.

Warehouse Books Inc.

www.warehousebooksinc.com

General categories, including children's, cooking, crafts, and military. Some music remainders, including sheet music, CDs, cassettes, VHS, and more.

World Publications, Inc.

www.wrldpub.net

Remainder and promotional books in all genres except textbooks and mass market.

RAID OUTLET STORES FOR RESALE PROFITS

If you know what you're looking for, you can find great merchandise for resale at outlets, sometimes called "factory stores" from the days when such stores, connected with factories, sold overruns, last year's fashions, or flawed items, or "seconds." Originally, outlets were simply a perk for company employees, and gradually they were opened to the public. Now they're big business: Outlets are the fastest-growing sector in the retail and travel industries, and are the No. 1 tourist destination among U.S. consumers.

Outlet centers are usually in the suburbs, where land is cheaper, and the merchandise doesn't compete with full-price retail stores near big cities. If you live within a couple hours' driving distance of a big outlet center, it can be well worth the trip.

As outlets have become more commonplace, their great deals have become rarer, for a variety of reasons:

- With the proliferation of imported goods, not as many factory seconds reach U.S. stores anymore.

- Retailers have gotten better at predicting demand, so overruns are not as plentiful.

- Today about 80 percent of the merchandise at outlet centers is manufactured just for the outlet, so the true bargain-basement stuff is harder to find.

To take one typical example, at an outlet apparel store you might see a table of sweaters with $100 price tags "marked down" to $40. But in many cases, the outlet planned to sell the sweaters for $40 all along—the original price tag is just an inflated "reference price" used to lure shoppers who don't know exactly what items are worth. If you're the typical tourist who doesn't shop for sweaters frequently, you might think the $40 offer is a fantastic deal.

Some outlet stores bend over backward to obfuscate the real value of items on sale, their origins, or exclusivity. Chico's has an "outlet brand" called Additions. Ralph Lauren operates "Polo" (overstock) and "Ralph Lauren" (more expensive) outlets. Outlets run by Gap, Izod and some higher-end brands carry merchandise made only for outlets, while others carry a blend of original and outlet-only merchandise. In many cases, when a brand's outlet line seems bargain-priced, it's mainly because the outlet goods are inferior to items carried in the company's regular stores and department stores. For example, Coach Inc., a maker of luxury bags, purses, and other items, generates about $2 billion in annual sales, with most of its profit generated by lower-end pieces sold in its outlets.

When comparing identical items, outlet prices are often about the same as "sale" prices at downtown department stores. On the other hand, the clearance racks at outlets contain some unbelievable buys. So, don't forget to browse the back of the store, because the merchandise there is seen by fewer shoppers, and usually has been marked down more than once.

Outlet merchandise, particularly apparel, can be a challenge for re-sellers. You certainly don't want to mistakenly pass off factory seconds as first-quality merchandise. Outlets frequently cut the label out of such garments to prevent them from being returned to stores for a full-price refund or credit. Sometimes the tags will contain the letter F, for "factory outlet." If you're in any doubt as to the origin or quality of outlet merchandise, ask the sales staff. If merchandise doesn't look like it just came off the rack at a department store, it's a good idea to sell it as a "used" item, even if it's never been worn.

Coupons are another way that outlets encourage people to spend, so view them with skepticism. Big outlet centers often sell a book of coupons that entitle you to additional discounts or free items, but experienced shoppers complain that they're rarely worth the money. Not all the stores at an outlet will participate, and the free items are usually worthless. For example, let's say after you buy five items you get a "free" clock radio. Sometimes the coupons are only redeemable on purchases over $100. This is just another technique the stores use to encourage people to spend money. Once shoppers have purchased the book of coupons, they feel like they have to buy something to justify their shopping trip, a concept known as "sunk costs." Don't ignore coupons entirely, but if you're buying for resale, it usually doesn't make any sense to spend your cash on coupons. It's a simple rule many resellers observe: Don't spend money to save money.

For me, one of the main draws of outlet centers is that they often include two or three of the major off-price retailers like TJ Maxx, Tuesday Morning, Ross, or HomeGoods in the same complex, or at a nearby location. These stores carry items from manufacturers that don't operate their own outlet stores.

The magazine *Consumer Reports* gave good reviews to many outlet stores in a 2006 report. After evaluating 33 popular outlet brands for value, quality, selection and service, the magazine gave top marks to Lenox, L.L. Bean, Mikasa, and OshKosh B'gosh. Survey respondents noted that VF Outlets (apparel), Coach (handbags and accessories), Lenox and Pfaltzgraff (dinnerware), and Saks Off 5th (clothing) offered "exceptional" discounts over the prices charged at regular stores for those brands. Of course, the survey results were based on perceptions of the consumers who responded, so take the results with a grain of salt.

Hassles for resellers of brand-name goods

Some brands that operate outlet stores discourage people from reselling their merchandise. Among the most notorious in this vein are Pottery Barn and Coach, which sometimes go as far as ejecting consumers from the store who are known to resell items on eBay or Amazon. Resellers get irritated at such policies, decrying them as unfair "discrimination." The resellers argue that the whole point of an outlet store is to sell as much merchandise as possible, at whatever price is on the price tags. After all, the resellers are performing a service—finding bargains for people who don't have the time and inclination to hunt for bargains at outlets themselves. But some retailers don't see it this way—they argue that online reselling "cheapens" their brand.

To avoid such problems, some resellers don't volunteer that they're buying merchandise for resale. For example, when I shop at a Ross or TJ Maxx where I've never been before, and wheel my cart up to the register overflowing with toys, the checkout clerk often gives me a wink and says something like, "Your kids are so lucky, look at all these toys!" I just smile and nod. If they knew I was reselling the toys at a 300 percent markup, they might not be so sweet about it—not that it's any of their business. On the other hand, at my regular haunts, where I know reselling is encouraged, I open a business account and provide a copy of my state resale certificate, exempting me from state sales tax on items bought for resale. More on that later.

As mentioned previously, makers of luxury goods typically don't like to see their merchandise resold online by independent sellers. For example, Coach Inc. has been known to aggressively pursue eBay sellers who auction its items. In 2010, after Seattle resident Gina Kim, a former Coach employee, auctioned the purse she bought for $428 with her employee discount, Coach erroneously reported her to eBay for selling counterfeit items. Despite the fact she did nothing untoward, Kim received a "cease and desist" letter accusing her of selling knockoffs, her eBay account was closed, and she was threatened with $2 million in fines and ordered to sign a statement admitting guilt. To top it all off, Coach's law firm asked Kim to pay $300 to avoid a lawsuit over the matter. Instead, Kim sued Coach for defamation and violation of state consumer-protection laws. Her suit claims that instead of detecting counterfeit merchandise, Coach is actually trying to thwart legitimate independent sellers of its bags, thereby forcing consumers to pay higher prices directly to Coach to obtain its goods.

"If Coach wants to send letters threatening $2 million lawsuits against their own customers, they should at least do minimal investigation to see whether those claims are accurate," says Jay Carlson, Kim's attorney. He's investigating whether more online merchants got similar threats from Coach, and simply paid the $300 to avoid litigation. Coach has denied the allegations, and vowed to "vigorously defend the claims" in court.

Tiffany & Co. has sent similar threatening letters to eBay merchants, postmarked from the same law firm used by Coach. Separately, Tiffany battled eBay in federal court for seven years, accusing the auction company of facilitating sales of counterfeit Tiffany items. Tiffany lost the case, and the U.S. Supreme Court declined to review that decision in 2010.

Many more companies have pressured eBay when sellers simply use stock photos of the brand's items without authorization from the company. Even when a seller isn't suspected of offering knock-offs, eBay usually deletes an auction after receiving a manufacturer's complaint. The automated procedure, which eBay calls the Verified Rights Owner (Vero) program, results in thousands of canceled auctions—and confusion among sellers and bidders—without even cursory investigations. In my opinion, based on anecdotes from a variety of sellers, such problems are more rare at Amazon, perhaps because Amazon itself is a major seller of brand-name goods, while eBay is merely a platform for independent sellers, with no retail operation of its own.

Fortunately, most stores are happy to sell as much as possible to anyone who opens their wallet. They appreciate that resellers are usually among their biggest customers, so these folks go out of their way to be helpful. Some will even let you know when new merchandise has arrived in the back room.

Insider tips for outlet store shopping

In this interview, Priscilla Ramsey, a professional shopper and online fashion reseller, shares tips for finding profitable items for resale at outlet and factory stores.

What's your advice on outlet shopping?

Go during the middle of the week, Tuesday or Wednesday. During the weekends, outlets are a zoo—they're overrun with tourists.

Like anyplace else, check about the payment and return policies for any outlets you shop at. They differ widely, and that can affect your buying strategy. Ironically, the nonreturnable stuff is often the best deal.

This isn't rocket science. You've just got to know your market and then you'll recognize the value. It helps to specialize.

Don't think you're automatically getting a deal just because it's a famous label and it's "marked down" 50 percent. Outlets are a profit center for the brands; they're not running a charity. Ann Taylor, Brooks Brothers, Donna Karan—all the famous names mix in junk that was made especially for outlets. You can't resell that stuff profitably. Do your homework, and don't buy anything unless you know the demand for an item and its going price.

What about the quality of outlet items, is it up to snuff?

Yes, one of the knocks against outlet merchandise is that it's subpar, and 80 or 90 percent of the time, that's a fact. For example, the buttons won't be as nice, there's not as much detail, or the material isn't of the same quality as the best things in department stores. To make money reselling fashion, you've got to know the merchandise—recognize the quality of a dress by running the material through your fingers, seeing the quality of the cut by watching how the piece hangs. When you know your market cold, you know what's a screaming buy, and what to pass on.

What about hard goods? Is this something outlet shoppers should target?

Hardware and appliances are a possibility, but they have their own minefields. If you don't know what you're doing, you might think that something is brand-new, but it has cosmetic flaws, or was used and returned, then reconditioned at a factory. This is something you'd need to disclose to your buyers, and of course, it would affect the sales price. You can't represent reconditioned merchandise as "new" merchandise.

Does the item carry the full manufacturer's warranty? You've got to keep track of all that.

Are you saying that outlets are a scam?

They're an opportunity, just like everything else. All retail, all advertising, is a scam at some level. Outlet shopping is entertainment for most people, and for them, it's probably safer than Vegas.

It depends on the store. Some outlets are true clearance centers, where you'll find bargains, while some are actually manufacturer's showcases, which are built to display full lines of merchandise, with no discounting whatsoever—I can't bother with those. The worst outlets sell only authorized knockoffs of their best pieces, and those aren't worth a visit, either.

Most of the people who buy from me know they're really getting a deal, and that's how I make money long-term. I get lots of repeat buyers.

The value of outlets is that they aggregate a tremendous amount of merchandise in one arena. But a really shrewd shopper, someone who does this full-time, can beat the outlet prices downtown, without driving out of your way. Seriously, I can usually beat outlet prices in the department stores, and I don't have to sift through as much of the crap made just for outlets.

What's your buying strategy?

I look for the stuff I like, and what my clients ask for—designer clothes and high-end purses and bags. It's a simple system: I look for top-quality stuff that's been marked 50 percent off retail, then marked down an additional 30, 40 percent from there.

Will you buy seconds, something with cosmetic damage?

Sure, if it has an additional markdown, and the flaw is virtually imperceptible.

Where do you resell?

My main business is selling directly to my clients as a personal shopper. As a sideline, I resell some of my discoveries online. When I expanded to online six years ago, I sold on eBay exclusively. Three years ago I got started on Amazon, and during that time my eBay volume has gone way down. Amazon has a better clientele, at least for what I'm selling. eBay's customers are a royal pain in the ass. I've never seen so many people who try to get something for nothing. I never hear from my Amazon customers, except when they thank me.

The main problem with Amazon is that you need an exact barcode match, which can be a show-stopper in clothing. So I maintain my eBay account and use it as a backup site, to clear out the stuff I can't return. eBay can be a good clearance venue.

What are your favorite stores?

Neiman Marcus Last Call has nice things, and when it's marked down you'll find good buys. The regular prices are just OK. Saks Fifth Avenue outlets can have a few good items, if you're willing to sort through all the rubbish. The clearance sections of Johnston & Murphy outlets are worth going through with a fine-tooth comb. It's a gold mine if you know how to recognize high-end stuff. VF Outlets has good pricing, but the brands aren't too exciting.

What outlets do you ignore totally?

J. Crew, Banana Republic, and Gap outlets are a waste of my time, since they only carry garments made for the outlets. I don't even go to those places when I'm shopping for myself.

Any final words of wisdom?

Take a calculator, so if you're checking out with a big load, you know what the total should be. When stuff has multiple markdowns, you'd be surprised how often it gets screwed up at the register. If you don't point out the mistake quickly, the clerk will run the incorrect total on your card before you realize it. As you might imagine, the error is usually in the store's favor.

Are they trying to rip you off? I doubt, it, but it's funny how seldom the error at the register is in your favor.

TOOLS:

USE AUTO-REPRICING AND LISTING TOOLS

After your online selling business reaches a certain level, you might need one or two more tools to remain as efficient and profitable as possible. But don't worry—having too much business is a good problem to have.

If you have lots of items listed at online marketplaces like Amazon, you'll improve your sales by keeping your prices adjusted according to competing offers. Sometimes this involves cutting your price, when demand for an item sinks, but sometimes you'll be able to raise prices.

When you list new inventory at competitive prices, a portion of it will sell promptly, then the other items typically sell much more slowly. "I sell about 42 percent [of new inventory] within the first 30 days," said Paul Hanrahan, a secondhand book dealer who calls his business MythReal Enterprises. "Then the rest goes much slower, in drips and drabs."

To keep the sales of your older listings as brisk and profitable as possible, it pays to monitor your prices and compare them against competitors. Exactly how you price and reprice is up to you. You might decide to sell at a loss sometimes, or hold out for the high price. Some sellers subscribe to the "fast nickel" strategy, while others like the "slow dime." Sometimes, it just depends. But don't kid yourself—if you're losing money on most transactions, you can't "make it up on volume"—or you'll go bankrupt eventually.

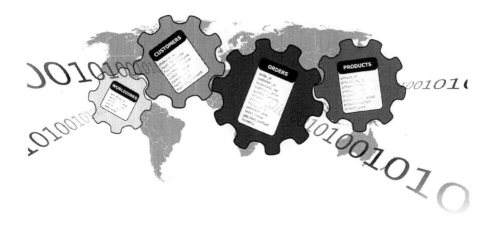

At first, when you've got only a few dozen or a couple hundred listings, it's easy enough to monitor everything by browsing your seller account on the Web. But after your business grows and the proportion of your mature, slower-moving inventory expands, adjusting prices can become a mind-numbing chore. For example, in my early selling years, before automated repricers were available, I had about 14,000 items listed on Amazon, and repricing them required three full days of painstaking work each time I did it—clicking back and forth between an endless series of Web pages, and typing in my revised numbers. By the time I'd get halfway done, I'd usually made a couple dozen mistakes and was ready to scream. Now I use a repricing tool to revise my listings to perfection three times a day, according to predetermined criteria, even while I sleep.

The tools listed below enable you to automate your repricing, as well as some other tasks including printing packing slips, invoices, address labels, and postage. Some of the services are designed to work only with Amazon, while others enable you to list the same inventory on multiple marketplaces. For example, you might use one of these tools to list each of your items on Amazon, eBay and Half.com simultaneously. When an item sells, it's deleted from the inventory listing for the other sites. Although such a setup is more complicated to set up, it can improve your cash flow. The tool you prefer will depend on what kind of business you have. Fortunately, you can try most of them for free on a trial basis.

It is possible that Amazon will develop a repricing tool of its own, perhaps a free one, since it has surveyed merchants on the topic recently. If this occurs, I will report the details at my website:

www.MyBarcodeBooty.com

Listtee.com. This service automates the listing of items for sale through Amazon's FBA program. The Web interface can be used with a barcode scanner. After you register your account, the first 50 listings are free each month, then pricing starts at $19.95 for up to 500 listings.

http://www.listtee.com/

RepriceIt.com. This Web-based tool allows you to specify 25 repricing parameters for Amazon inventory, such as "match the lowest competing price" or "add $5 to the lowest competing price." There's also an automatic repricer which will try to optimally reprice your merchandise, while ignoring certain factors, like sellers with low feedback and unreasonable "lowball" prices. The monthly fee ranges from $9.95 for sellers with up to 500 listings, to $74.95 for sellers with up to 100,000 listings.

https://www.repriceit.com

Aman for Amazon Sellers. Aman is software for your desktop PC that automates a variety of tasks for Amazon sellers. In addition to repricing, Aman can dramatically reduce the time you spend performing repetitive tasks, such as generating packing slips, pick lists, postage labels. The software helps you track your inventory and automate your listing and repricing procedures. It's constantly updated as the features on Amazon change.

http://spaceware.com/

More service providers are listed here:

http://aws.amazon.com/customerapps/Amazon-Sellers?browse=1

Online postage

If you're performing any fulfillment yourself, you can probably speed up your operation with an online postage service. If it saves you the headache of standing in line at the Post Office twice a week, it can be worth the monthly fee 100 times over. Here are two recommendations:

www.endicia.com

www.stamps.com

Heavy-duty services for mega-sellers. Amazon and eBay sellers who have a big, complicated business—or integrate their online selling with a brick-and-mortar store, and don't have an e-commerce programmer on their staff—have a few more options:

http://www.channeladvisor.com

http://www.monsoonworks.com

http://fillz.com/

These companies provide special solutions for big companies, and they're relatively expensive. They might not say exactly how much they'll charge you until they've got you on the phone.

Like my mom says, "If you need to ask the price, you can't afford it."

SALES:

STAKE OUT THE BEST SALES PLATFORM

OK, now you know where to get your inventory. Now, where can you sell it at the best prices?

You can sell your wares anywhere you wish—at a flea market, door-to-door, in a kiosk at your local mall, from the trunk of your car, on your own website. But the most efficient, profitable method, especially for beginners with limited time and capital, is by opening a third-party selling account at an established Internet marketplace, like eBay and Amazon. For selling on their U.S. sites, you'll need to be of legal age and have a U.S. bank account and a credit or debit card.

This section lists recommended sites for standard consumer goods, and is not focused on handmade items or crafts. Here are brief introductions to the best options, and a link to information about creating seller accounts, listing your items, and rules and regulations.

Amazon.com. Increasingly, Amazon is a top choice for entrepreneurs selling a variety of goods. Amazon has nearly 100 million registered buyers. You can sell on Amazon with no up-front investment. After your sales, you'll pay miscellaneous fees and a commission of 6 percent to 15 percent depending on the product category.

Some sellers decide to sell only on Amazon, as a way to keep things simple. Others list the same inventory simultaneously on Amazon and other sites. This creates some extra administrative work, but there are automated solutions described in the next section. For more information:

http://www.amazon.com/gp/seller/sell-your-stuff.html

Also, Amazon has a series of video tutorials that demonstrate, step-by-step, the processes of listing items for sale, managing orders, providing customer service, and handling returns, refunds and customer feedback. Although the tutorials focus on bookselling, the principles apply to other product categories as well:

http://www.amazon.com/gp/help/customer/display.html ?nodeId=200270440#webinars

eBay.com. Like Amazon, eBay has millions of registered users. Unlike Amazon, eBay doesn't sell anything itself; it only provides a platform for independent merchants. Most of its transactions are auctions lasting one week, but a growing number of transactions are at fixed prices, which eBay calls "Buy it Now." Listing your items for sale on eBay is more complicated compared with Amazon, and its fee structure is a bit more complicated.

In its heyday several years ago, eBay was a Mecca for independent sellers, sole proprietors and Mom-and-Pop shops alike. But in recent years, growth at eBay has stalled, while Amazon has been booming. Experts have a couple of theories as to why Amazon has recently grown faster:

- As online commerce has matured, consumers have migrated away from the online auction format eBay is famous for. Most buyers aren't shopping for a collectible. Most aren't even looking for a rock-bottom deal. They just want to quickly find the stuff they're looking for. They want to know how much they'll pay for it, and when they'll get it.

- A different breed of buyer inhabits Amazon, generally speaking. They quibble less, pay faster, and generally create fewer headaches than eBay buyers. In many categories, sellers report higher prices and brisker sales at Amazon than at eBay.

Unless the item for sale is a collectible or hand-made, auctions are a turnoff for many shoppers because they're forced to wait, competing against each other for the low price. With a fixed-price marketplace like Amazon, sellers compete against each other, mainly on price and reputation. Sure, eBay has fixed-price listings in addition to auctions, and it has millions of active buyers. It's well worth exploring, and many sellers offer their wares on both sites. But many buyers prefer the standardized, efficient buying process on Amazon. Bottom line: From a seller's point of view, in the competition of online marketplaces, Amazon is currently winning the battle by delivering more buyers with bigger wallets.

Fairly or unfairly, eBay has also gotten a reputation in some quarters as a conduit for counterfeit merchandise. I'm sure the vast majority of transactions are above board. But product manufacturers—especially those that don't want their items discounted online—are often successful in getting eBay to cancel auctions for their merchandise by simply accusing the seller of offering knock-offs. As a result, honest eBay merchants can find it difficult to offer famous brands on the site. More on this in the chapter "Raid Outlet Stores for Resale Profits."

For more information on getting started at eBay:

http://pages.ebay.com/sellerinformation/howtosell/selli ngbasics.html

Half.com. Half.com is a division of eBay dedicated to media products like new and used books, textbooks, videos, music, videogames and game systems. Like eBay, Half doesn't sell new merchandise itself, but serves as a platform for independent merchants. Transactions are handled at fixed prices, with no auctions. If you are getting started selling media items, Half.com may be a good option because you can arrange for your listings to appear on eBay too at no additional cost.

http://pages.half.ebay.com/help/seller/createacct_sell.html

Bonanza.com. Formerly known as "Bonanzle," this site offers an "easy" alternative to eBay. There's not as much selling activity as eBay and Amazon, but sales are on the rise. Worth a look.

https://www.bonanza.com/booths/sell_splash

Buy.com. Somewhat like Amazon, Buy.com sells a variety of new merchandise, and also operates a marketplace for independent sellers. Unlike Amazon and eBay, Buy.com carefully screens new sellers, and accepts only those with a proven track record at an online marketplace or a dedicated e-commerce website. Buy.com has only a fraction of the buying activity at Amazon and eBay, but it has big plans. Buy has expanded its categories and third-party merchant programs, and in

2010 was acquired by Rakuten Inc., Japan's largest e-commerce company.

http://www.buy.com/loc/marketplace-landing/67274.html

Facebook. It's not well known as an e-commerce platform, but as one of the world's most-visited websites, it's hard to ignore Facebook Marketplace. Some people like the idea of selling items to friends, and others don't. This is one that probably isn't immediately useful, but it bears watching. Sometimes it pays to be early to the party.

http://apps.facebook.com/marketplace

Barnes & Noble. This chain bookseller enables independent merchants to sell used and collectible media on its website, too.

http://www.barnesandnoble.com/used/help/authsell.asp ?PID=33499

ABEbooks.com. ABEBooks, formerly known as Advanced Book Exchange, is an international marketplace for books. Independent sellers offer their used books, many are rare or out-of-print, and the site is increasing its sales of new books. The company was acquired by Amazon in 2008.

http://www.abebooks.com/books/Sell

Alibris.com. Like ABEbooks, Alibris is an international online marketplace catering to buyers of used and rare books and other media supplied by independent sellers.

http://www.alibris.com/sellers/help

Craiglist.com. This can be a viable channel for trading goods that are difficult or expensive to ship. Some sellers use Craigslist as a free method of finding inventory. Remember that transacting in cash with unfamiliar people can be time-consuming and dangerous.

http://www.craigslist.org/about/help

Seller profile: Sue Johnson

Sue is an online dealer of used and collectible books near the Twin Cities in Minnesota:

How and when did you get involved with online selling?

In 2001, my husband and I were beginning the process of looking for a smaller home now that the children had left home. At the time, I was a consultant working at home. As I looked around, thinking about a move, I noted that we were overrun by books—both of us being avid readers. A thought occurred to me, "I buy used books on Amazon, so how do I sell used books on Amazon?"

I signed up as an Amazon seller, listed 12 books as a trial run, and they all sold in less than a day, except for two. I continued to list books as a means of weeding out before a move.

Since we had always attended Friends of the Library sales in the Twin Cities area, to get more books for us and the children, we continued to attend as a means of making extra money—at that point this was "fun money." I continued to consult and sell books, while my husband held a full-time job. We moved to a smaller home, and by now I had more than 1,200 books online. I was hooked—how can a bibliophile resist being around all of those books?

In 2005, my husband had a stroke—one of three he suffered during the following three years. He is now disabled, lost his job in 2007, and so he works with me full-time finding, listing, selling, packing, and mailing books. It was also at this point, I stopped consulting and began working at this full-time.

What is your favorite type of book to sell?

I sell mostly nonfiction—and recently started dipping into the First Edition collectibles.

When I started there was no such thing as "scouting tools," so I learned this business by trial and error. I learned quickly what may sell, and what may not. I now generally stay away from ex-library books, unless they have a very low ranking, are in very good condition, and there is a market for them (cookbooks being one genre). I recently picked up 12 cookbooks at a library sale, and they were all sold within a week.

So, scanning alone is no guarantee of success?

No. Many sellers I see at book sales are simply scanning barcodes. From experience, I can scan a table of books with my eyes, and take the ones I know are likely to be decent sellers. Sometimes, I feel badly for these sellers—other times I am glad they are without a clue, as it allows me to take what they leave behind.

Sellers should understand that this is a lifelong learning experience if they want to be successful. Loving books is immensely helpful.

Scanning is only one tool—your mind is the most important one.

What selling platforms do you use? Which do you prefer?

I sell on Amazon, Alibris, ABE, Half and Biblio. Ninety percent of my inventory is books, with occasional DVDs. Amazon accounts for approximately 70 percent of my sales, Alibris has 25 percent, with the remainder spread among the other venues.

What else do you enjoy about online bookselling?

I take pride in maintaining positive feedback, shipping books daily, responding to inquiries, refunding when I missed something, and providing a positive buyer experience. I know, as a reader, how hard it is to buy a book without being able to see or touch it.

So, I go to lengths to describe as well as I can every little tear, any underlining, highlighting, smudge marks, etc.

My son and son-in-law are both booksellers now. I trained both of them. My son has been selling for five years, and my son-in-law for two years now that he is a stay-at-home dad. They have learned how to appreciate books, are professional, respectful of other sellers, and find joy in the hunt.

What kind of pricing tools do you use?

I use MediaScouter, mainly to check my work as well as sales rankings, and whether a book remains saleable, etc. I spend over an hour a day looking at books online, seeing what others have to sell, and checking my "gut" against reality.

Some worry about sales erosion due to e-books and Kindle.

I am so weary of the gloom and doom. There will always be readers who want to hold the book—count me as one of them. I cannot see the e-readers working as cookbooks, how-to books, etc. My daughter takes the bus into work and sees many people, from many walks of life, on each bus trip. She says there are one or two e-readers among 10 or 15 people who are reading books.

I sell an average of 400 to 475 books a month. Sales have increased, even while my inventory has decreased as I increase prices and weed out the less lucrative books.

Is Fulfillment by Amazon viable for your business?

It probably is, but I just have not taken the step, and not sure if I will. I have a number of bookseller friends here in the Twin Cities who now use it and like it.

FULFILLMENT:

OUTSOURCE YOUR FULFILLMENT

This chapter might also be called "Getting rid of your dirty work." Really, it's about being efficient.

With the default method of Amazon selling, sellers ship items directly to buyers, often through the Postal Service. With this method, the customer pays your sales price and a shipping fee, which you apply toward your costs of postage and packing materials. Amazon credits the proceeds to your bank account, minus its seller fees and commission.

By contrast, with Fulfillment by Amazon, sellers ship their items to an Amazon warehouse, where they're stored until purchased. In exchange for extra fees, FBA handles your warehousing, customer service, shipping, and returns. In addition to the time savings, a big plus with FBA is that your listings qualify for Amazon's free shipping offers, just as buyers expect when ordering new merchandise directly from Amazon. Generally, buyers qualify for free "Super Saver" shipping when they spend $25 or more, and subscribers of "Amazon Prime," which costs about $80 a year, always get free two-day shipping—except on purchases of non-FBA merchandise.

Fulfillment by Amazon. With FBA, participating sellers ship part or all of their inventory to one of several Amazon Fulfillment Centers scattered across the United States. When shipping FBA items to Amazon, sellers can take advantage of a discounted rate through United Parcel Service. Depending on the size of your shipment and the distance to the warehouse, shipments will cost you approximately 20 cents to 50 cents per pound, which is a substantial discount from the

UPS regular rate. The shipping labels can be generated through Amazon's website, and the cost is deducted from your account.

FBA doesn't necessarily lock you into selling on Amazon exclusively, or at all. In other words, you could list items for sale on eBay or your own website, and have those orders handled via FBA's "basic fulfillment" service. More on that later.

Costs of FBA vs. self-fulfillment. Amazon has a variety of miscellaneous fees that apply to each FBA transaction. There are "pick and pack" fees, a weight-based fee, and storage fees—and all of these are on top of regular Amazon selling fees and commission. Specifically, Amazon charges a storage fee, by the cubic foot, for each item you have at their warehouse. Each day, Amazon calculates your cubic-foot usage, and the total fee is deducted from your account once per month. In general, one way to look at FBA is that it adds another 5 percent or 10 percent to your regular Amazon fees. On the other hand, FBA adds to your sales volume, and you can usually charge a few dollars more for your items compared with non-FBA sellers due to the free shipping factor. Some FBA sellers report that the program saves them enough money on postage, insurance and refunds for lost packages to cover all their FBA costs. On top of that, they're outsourcing much of the labor and administrative headaches.

Let's examine a typical transaction, the sale of a book weighing about 2.5 pounds. Here are the exact figures from a recent FBA transaction from my Amazon seller account:

Carmine's Family-Style Cookbook
Product charges (sales price): $16.95

Amazon fees:
Commission: $-2.54
FBA per unit fulfillment fee (pick & pack) : $-0.50
FBA weight based fee: $-0.96
Variable closing fee: $-1.35

Transaction Total: $11.60

Pre-transaction inventory costs:

Book acquisition: -$3.80

Inbound shipping (Sending to FBA warehouse via UPS): -$0.40

Monthly storage fees at FBA warehouse: -$0.02

So, I netted $7.38 on this transaction, not too shabby. Unfortunately, not all transactions turn out favorably. If your selling price is too low, you might end up paying more in inventory costs and selling fees than you realize from the sale. Of course, this can happen whether you're using FBA or not.

Amazon has a handy online calculator that enables you to calculate how profitable a potential inventory item is likely to be, and whether it's best to fulfill that item yourself, or use FBA. When signed into Amazon, navigate to this page:

https://sellercentral.amazon.com/gp/fbacalc/fba-calculator.html

To illustrate the calculator, I've plugged in the same book mentioned above (but you can use any product you're considering selling):

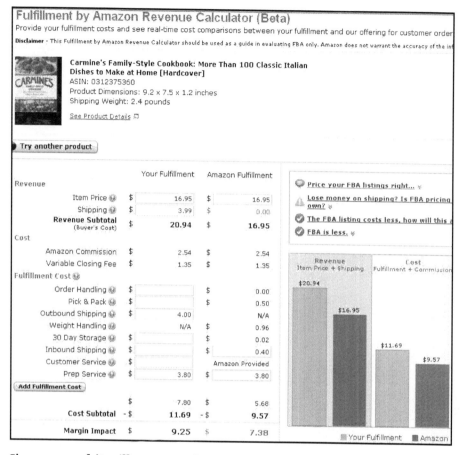

I've assumed it will cost me about $4 to package and ship the book to my buyer (shown in the "Outbound Shipping" box). I've shown my cost for acquiring the book, $3.80, in the "Prep Service" box.

As you can see with this example, I can clear a dollar and change more if I fulfill the order myself (shown on the bottom line, "Margin Impact"). But that's a bit misleading, for two reasons. First, with FBA, the buyer can qualify for free shipping—so they're potentially getting the book for $16.95 instead of $20.94, making it more likely I'll get the sale, and turn over my inventory faster. Secondly, I haven't included how much time it takes me to fulfill the order myself, and time is money. With self-fulfillment, I've got to find the book, package it, lug it to my car, and (heaven forbid) stand in line at the Post Office or UPS Store. Multiply that time by your number of sales per day, and it can add up to hours—time you can spend scouting for more inventory. Or going on vacation.

Another plus with FBA: those items get enhanced exposure on Amazon's offer listing page. Items are sorted so that FBA listings can appear near the top "low price" position, even though the seller's price might exceed the price of standard Marketplace listings. The difference is, Amazon automatically assumes "free shipping" as part of the price-sorting it presents to buyers. So in theory, FBA sellers can charge a few dollars more than non-FBA sellers, due to this "free shipping" advantage.

To illustrate, here's an Amazon Marketplace offer page, where you can see how an FBA item gets top billing over a lower-priced item fulfilled directly by the merchant. Buyers are accustomed to seeing the lowest-priced item on top, but in this case, "free" shipping is calculated into the sorting.

Outsourcing your day-to-day chores isn't the only advantage to FBA. For example, users typically sell their items faster—and sell a greater proportion of their listing (called "sell-through" by retailers) because FBA exposes your merchandise to buyers who typically don't buy from smaller, independent merchants. These additional customers include:

LOOK INSIDE!

The Home-Based Bookstore: Start Your Own Business Selling Used Books on Amazon, eBay or Your Own Web Site (Paperback)
by Steve Weber

Price at a Glance

List Price: ~~$18.95~~

Used: from $12.82

New: from $15.81

‹ Return to product information

Have one to sell? [Sell yours here]

| All | New (22 from $15.81) | Used (27 from $12.82) |

Show ⦿ All ○ *Prime* offers only   Sorted by [Price + Shipping ▼]

All 1-15 of 49 offers

Price + Shipping	Condition	Seller Information	Buying Options
$16.17 and eligible for *Prime*	Used - Good	Seller: **BooksandDreams** [FULFILLMENT BY AMAZON] Seller Rating: ★★★★★ **99% positive** over the past 12 months. (1,881 total ratings) In Stock. • $3.99 Overnight Shipping • Free Two-day Shipping	[Add to Cart] or Turn on 1-Click to use your Amazon Prime benefits.
$12.87 + $3.99 shipping	Used - Good	Seller: **WookieBooks** Seller Rating: ★★★★★ **99% positive** over the past 12 months. (648 total ratings) In Stock. Ships from TX, United States. Expedited shipping available.	[Add to Cart] or Sign in to turn on 1-Click ordering.
$17.05 and eligible for *Prime*	New	**amazon**.com. In Stock. • $3.99 Overnight Shipping: Get it Wednesday, February 2 (order within 5hr 22min) • Free Two-day Shipping: Get it Thursday, February 3 (order within 9hr 22min)	[Add to Cart] or Turn on 1-Click to use your Amazon Prime benefits.

- Buyers who make it a habit to only buy from Amazon directly, and avoid purchasing from third-party sellers. (Customers might behave this way for any number of reasons. Perhaps they don't trust third parties to handle the order with the same precision and speed as Amazon, or they've had a poor experience buying from an individual seller in the past. Perhaps the item is a gift, and the buyer doesn't want to take a chance on outside fulfillment or whether the item is truly "new." Sometimes the buyer wants the item gift-wrapped by Amazon.) Even when Marketplace sellers offer a much lower price than Amazon, a substantial portion of buyers still decide to pay more for the Amazon-fulfilled item.

- Price-sensitive shoppers who want to take advantage of Amazon free shipping offers. These buyers want to use Amazon's "Super Saver" free shipping deal on orders over $25, while others are members of "Amazon Prime," which entitles them to free two-day shipping and other perks. You'd be surprised how many people pay extra simply to get "free" shipping.

So FBA's connection to Amazon's free shipping deals can boost your sales substantially. According to sellers, at least one-third of Amazon buyers take advantage of Super Saver shipping or Prime discount shipping.

The bottom line is, FBA can be a great way for small sellers to expand. I have used it almost exclusively since 2009 and have been very satisfied with it. There are few alternatives—especially for single entrepreneurs who don't generate hundreds or thousands of orders per day—although eBay has said it's considering developing a similar service. There are several other fulfillment services with long, excellent track records. Shipwire.com is the alternative I hear about most often. But FBA is unique in that participating sellers get access to Amazon's huge customer base.

However, I can understand why some sellers who have a different type of business wouldn't be interested in FBA. For example, a bookseller specializing in super-expensive, rare volumes requiring extra-careful handling and special shipping will probably want to continue handling their business the same way they've been doing it.

Basic fulfillment. Earlier, I mentioned that you can sell your items stored at FBA on other venues, perhaps your own website or eBay store. Amazon calls this procedure "Basic Fulfillment." For these orders, Amazon passes the shipping cost to you, which varies according to the type of item and shipping method. You may offer three shipping speeds: standard delivery (5-7 days), two-day delivery, or next-day delivery.

In addition to the "shipping method" fee, Basic Fulfillment orders are also subject to the per-fulfillment and weight-based fees assessed on regular FBA orders. Basic Fulfillment is more expensive than the costs resulting from Amazon orders, so if you're considering it, you'll need to examine how Basic Fulfillment costs would affect your profitability.

Basic Fulfillment orders can be initiated in two ways:

- You, the seller, can submit an "order fulfillment request" to Amazon using a Web form or an uploaded file. In this case, you'd supply the buyer's shipping address and other instructions.

- Your customers can initiate the order through your website if the site supports FBA's system, which uses XML, a general-purpose Web formatting language.

Competitive advantages of FBA. Using FBA provides some important advantages to sellers. Buyers who are hesitant to purchase from a third party are more likely to purchase when they know the FBA order is being handled by Amazon directly, using the same pick, pack, and ship system. And there are other key advantages:

- FBA items are highlighted on Amazon's product pages with a logo emphasizing "Fulfilled by Amazon."

- FBA items are eligible for Amazon's free shipping deals—Super Saver Shipping and Prime shipping. That way, buyers can combine their Amazon and FBA items in the same shipment. Buyers can also choose one-day shipping.

- Listings can appear at the top of offer pages, in the "buy box" right along with Amazon's listing (nonmedia products only).

- Buyers can return FBA purchases directly to Amazon.

- You can take advantage of special promotions and variations.

- You can include your logo with the product description and on the offer listing page for nonmedia items.

FBA merchants can also qualify for "featured" merchant status in certain categories, providing even more visibility for your listings. Amazon doesn't disclose what criteria merchants must meet to obtain featured status, but apparently the program is linked to high sales volume, high feedback scores, and low refund rates.

You can get more information about FBA and enroll in the program by completing the Web form at this page:

http://www.amazonservices.com/fulfillment

After you accept the FBA agreement, you tell Amazon which products you want them to fulfill. You label your products and packages for shipping via UPS to an Amazon fulfillment center.

Also, FBA is a possible solution for non-U.S. sellers who want access to the American market. For example, sellers in Canada or elsewhere can ship their items to one of the U.S. fulfillment centers and let Amazon handle their U.S. distribution. To participate, the seller must have an Amazon.com seller account, which requires a U.S. bank account. Amazon has also launched FBA in the United Kingdom and Germany, which is used by sellers looking to expand their sales in Europe.

FBA disadvantages. Although FBA offers many advantages, you should consider the drawbacks. Among the most critical:

- You'll incur monthly storage fees for all items that don't sell. If you decide to remove the items from FBA, Amazon will charge fees for returning them or removing and disposing of the items.

- Items are outside your immediate control. If a potential buyer has a question about a certain aspect of an item, you might not be able to provide an answer since you can't pull the item from your shelf to inspect it.

- Loss of control over fulfillment. If Amazon fumbles your order, your customer will be unhappy. However, if you receive a negative feedback rating from a customer due to a delivery problem caused by Amazon, Seller Support will usually remove the negative rating from your overall feedback score.

For complete information about FBA and its fees, consult this section of Amazon's website:

http://fba.amazon.com

And Amazon maintains a forum for FBA sellers:

http://www.amazonsellercommunity.com/forums/forum .jspa?forumID=29&start=0

LEGAL:

KEEP YOUR BUSINESS LEGAL

Now, we get to the fine print, the stuff you need to stay legal. You didn't expect this entire book to be a bowl of cherries, did you?

Once you've decided to pursue sales, whatever the venue, you'll need to decide how your business will be formally organized and how you'll meet your tax obligations. As your business grows, you should periodically revisit the question of the best form of organization for your business.

● **Sole proprietorship.** Establishing a sole proprietorship is cheap and relatively simple. This term designates an unincorporated business that is owned by one individual, the simplest form of business organization to start and maintain. You are the sole owner and you take on all the business's liabilities and risks. You state the income and expenses of the business on your own tax return.

Any business that hasn't incorporated is automatically a sole proprietorship. So if you haven't incorporated, formed a partnership, or established a limited liability company, your business is a sole proprietorship by default.

The good news about a sole proprietorship is that you're entitled to all the profits from the business. On the other hand, you are 100 percent responsible for all debts and liabilities. So if your business is sued, your personal assets could be seized.

As a sole proprietorship, you're liable for paying income tax and self-employment tax (Social Security and Medicare taxes), and for filing quarterly estimated taxes based on your net income. Since you don't have an employer reporting your income and withholding a portion of your paycheck for taxes, you must inform the IRS about the income from your Amazon selling and make quarterly tax payments on the profits. Quarterly installments of the estimated tax, submitted with Form 1040-ES, are due April 15, June 15, September 15, and January 15 of the following calendar year. If you don't yet sell full-time and you also work at a job where your employer withholds income for taxes, you can ask your employer to increase your withholding. That way you might avoid having to mail in quarterly estimated payments on your profits.

As far as the IRS is concerned, a sole proprietorship and its owner are treated as a single entity. Business income and losses are reported with your personal tax return on Form 1040, Schedule C, "Profit or Loss From Business."

If you've never filed a Schedule C with the IRS before, you might wish to hire an accountant to assist you with the first year's return. The following year you might complete the return yourself. One helpful tool in this regard is tax-preparation software such as TurboTax or TaxCut. Unlike the IRS instruction pamphlets, these products guide you through the tax-filing process in plain English. The program can save you several hours at tax time because you don't have to decipher the arcane language of the IRS.

- **Partnership.** A partnership is the relationship between two or more persons who agree to operate a business. Each person contributes something toward the business and has a stake in its profits and losses. Partnerships must file an annual information return to report the income and deductions from operations. Instead of paying income tax, the partnership "passes through" profits or losses to the partners, and each partner includes their share of the income or loss on their tax return.

- **Corporation.** In a corporation, prospective shareholders exchange money or property for the corporation's stock. The corporation generally takes deductions similar to those of a sole proprietorship to calculate income and taxes. Corporations may also take special deductions.

- **Limited liability company.** A limited liability company (LLC) is a relatively new business structure allowed by state statute. LLCs are popular because owners have limited personal liability for the company's debts and actions, as is also the case for a corporation.

Local ordinances

Call your county government's headquarters to ask what types of permits and licenses are required for your business. Some cities, counties, and states require any business to get a business license. If you're working at home, your city or county may require a "home occupation permit" or a zoning variance, and you might have to certify that you won't have walk-in retail customers. Since your business is an online and mail-order business, this shouldn't be a problem.

If you are conducting your business under a trade name or your Amazon nickname, you should file a "fictitious name" certificate with your county or state government office so people who deal with your business can find out who the legal owner is. This is also known as a DBA name (Doing Business As) or an "assumed name."

Sales taxes. Although the Internet is a "tax-free zone" in many respects, this does not apply to state sales taxes for goods sold to customers in your state. To pay the tax, you'll need to open an account and obtain a "resale license," known as a resale number or sales tax certificate in some instances.

You don't collect state sales tax on orders shipped outside your state. Internet sales, as well as fax, telephone, and mail-order sales shipped to another state, aren't subject to sales tax unless you have an office or warehouse located there. In some states, shipping and handling fees are not subject to sales tax, but in some they are—you will need to investigate the issue for your home state. This is the way things operate today, but there's no guarantee it will stay this way.

Once you've made the decision that your business is no longer a hobby, obtain a resale certificate from your state tax office. This will relieve you of paying state sales tax on the items you buy for resale, but it will also obligate you to report and pay taxes on the sales you make to customers within your state.

A caveat: State sales tax is an evolving area you'll need to monitor. Because online sales are growing so rapidly, local governments are salivating at the prospect of collecting local sales taxes from online sellers, no matter where the item is shipped. Sooner or later, it's inevitable that sellers will be regulated and taxed more than they are today.

Income taxes. Your form of business determines which income tax return form you have to file. For the vast majority of sellers without employees or a walk-in store, a sole proprietorship makes the most sense. As noted previously, the other most common forms of business are partnerships, corporations, and limited liability companies.

Many beginning sellers spend lots of time dreaming about what they'll be able to "write off" on their tax return, now that they have a business. Actually, what you're doing is paying taxes on your net profits. Your write-offs are the costs of doing business, such as buying inventory and paying for postage. What's left over is the profit, and you pay income tax on that.

As far as the IRS is concerned, your business must become profitable within three years or it will be considered a hobby, and none of the expenses will be deductible. For example, your mileage traveling to estate sales where you pick up inventory is deductible for tax purposes. But don't rely on your memory to keep track of such expenses. Keep a notebook in your car to document the mileage and expenses for your buying trips. If you're ever audited, the IRS will want to see documentation for your travel and other deducted expenses.

To figure your taxes, you'll need to keep track of every penny involving your business. Keep receipts and records, and put your expenses into categories such as "postage," "shipping supplies," "inventory," and so on.

Your bookkeeping chores can be greatly simplified with financial software such as Quicken. Most banks offer free downloads of your transactions, and once you set it up, Quicken can automatically categorize all your business expenses and eliminate most of the headaches at tax time. If you have a debit or check card linked to your account, you can use the card for nearly all your business transactions. Those records can be downloaded into Quicken right along with your banking records, making your bookkeeping that much simpler.

If you're familiar with bookkeeping and accounting principles, you might be able to do a better job with QuickBooks software, which is designed especially for small-business accounting.

Another handy tool for keep track of your business income and expenses is Mint.com. Its free service enables you to download, categorize, and record transactions from most financial institutions and credit-card accounts.

Supporting documents. The law doesn't require any particular record-keeping technique, as long as you can plainly show your income and expenses. Your records must summarize your business transactions, showing your gross income, deductions, and credits. It's a good idea to have a separate checking account for your business so your personal funds are not included.

You should preserve the paper trail of any purchases, sales, and other transactions, including any invoices or receipts, sales slips, bills, deposit slips, and records of canceled checks. Keep documents that support your tax return organized and in a secure place. More detailed information is available in IRS Publication 583, "Starting a Business and Keeping Records," which is available here:

http://www.irs.gov/publications/p583/index.html

Reporting by online marketplaces. Starting in 2011, online marketplaces such as eBay, Half.com and Amazon began providing sellers and the Internal Revenue Service with a summary of their selling activity, which is detailed on an IRS Form 1099-K. The practice began with transactions occurring on or after Jan. 1, 2011. It's the result of new IRS regulations that require online marketplaces to generate the forms for sellers with more than 200 transactions and $20,000 in sales during the year.

Your Form 1099-Ks will show a consolidated report of all payments received from each company such as eBay or Amazon where you made sales. This information is also reported as gross income to the IRS.

The new rules apply to everyone, including part-time sellers and those with more than one small account. For sellers with multiple accounts, the marketplaces combine all of them to calculate your volume status. For example, sellers close to or exceeding the IRS thresholds by the end of the 2011 calendar year would receive 1099-Ks in early 2012.

According to eBay, sellers who don't meet the IRS thresholds probably will receive no Form 1099-K for the year, and no transactions will be reported to the IRS for that year.

Business use of your home. You may be able to deduct expenses related to the business use of parts of your home. This deduction is subject to certain requirements and doesn't include expenses such as mortgage interest and real estate taxes.

To qualify to claim expenses for business use of your home, you must use part of your home exclusively and regularly as your principal place of business or for storage. This means the area used for your business must be a room or other separate identifiable space, but you are not required to designate the space by a permanent wall or partition.

There are some exceptions to the "exclusive use" test. If you use part of your home for storage of inventory, you can claim expenses for the business use of your home without meeting the exclusive use test — but you must meet these criteria:

- You keep the inventory in your home for use in your business.

- Your home is your business's only fixed location.

- You use the storage space on a regular basis.

- The space used for storage is a separately identifiable space suit-able for storage.

To qualify under the regular use test, you must use a specific area of your home for business on a regular basis. "Incidental" or "occasional" business use is not regular use as far as the IRS is concerned.

Insurance. Home-based businesses aren't usually covered under a regular homeowners or renter's insurance policy. If inventory items are stolen or damaged, it's probably not covered. If a delivery person or customer is injured at your home, you may be liable unless an "endorsement" or "rider" is added to your homeowner or renter's policy. The cost of the additional premium is usually quite low for a business without employees or a huge inventory, so it's well worth considering.

Bookkeeping. For a small Amazon business, simple "cash basis" bookkeeping should suffice. The cash method entails recording income when money is received and expenses as they are paid. "Cash basis" does not necessarily mean your transactions are in cash, but refers to checks, money orders, and electronic payments as well as currency. If you're not familiar with the basics of bookkeeping, read "Small Time Operator: How to Start Your Own Business, Keep Your Books, Pay Your Taxes and Stay Out of Trouble" by Bernard Kamoroff.

Cash accounting is simpler to understand and use than the other type of bookkeeping, accrual accounting. Businesses are allowed to use cash accounting if annual sales are below $1 million.

Hiring employees. The decision to begin hiring employees is a big step for any business. Although employees can enable you to expand your selling and profits, hiring will add tremendously to your paperwork and the extent to which your business is regulated by the government. Having employees means that you need to keep payroll records and withhold income, Social Security, and state taxes, as well as Medicare and worker's compensation insurance. The states and the IRS require timely payroll tax returns and strict observance of employment laws. Penalties are usually swift and severe for failure to pay payroll taxes.

An Amazon seller struggling with a busy workload might be tempted to pay cash "under the table" for help instead of actually hiring employees during their transition from a one-person shop to employer status. Don't do it. There is no gray area here—such practices are illegal because payroll taxes and worker's compensation insurance aren't being paid.

An alternative to taking on employees is to hire independent outside contractors. You can hire contractors as needed, and the practice entails less paperwork and none of the headaches of paying employment taxes or producing payroll tax returns.

If you hire an independent contractor, make certain the person doing the work understands completely that they are not an employee. Numerous small-business owners have gotten into scrapes with state and federal regulators when their independent contractors were later denied unemployment compensation or were found not to have paid their own Social Security taxes. Also, be aware that the IRS has been tightening up its rules on which types of workers can be considered independent contractors.

Index